# WHEN FOOD BECOMES YOUR ENEMY

GW00729177

# WHEN FOOD BECOMES YOUR ENEMY

*Anorexia Nervosa, Bulimia Nervosa
and Comfort Eating*

GILLIAN MOORE-GROARKE

SYLVIA THOMPSON

MERCIER PRESS

MERCIER PRESS
PO Box 5, 5 French Church Street, Cork
16 Hume Street, Dublin 2

© G. Moore-Groarke & S. Thompson

ISBN 1 85635 109 2

*A CIP for this book is available from the British Library*

10 9 8 7 6 5 4 3 2 1

*This book is sold subject to the condition that it shall not, by way of trade or otherwise, be lent, resold, hired out or otherwise circulated without the publisher's prior consent in any form of binding or cover other than that in which it is published and without a similar condition including this condition being imposed on the subsequent purchaser.*

*Printed in Ireland by Colour Books Ltd.*

# CONTENTS

*To the sufferers of eating disorders everywhere*


We are born crying;
We often live complaining;
But do not die disappointed.

# ACKNOWLEDGEMENTS

The authors would like to thank the following people who helped in various ways towards this book: Sr Gregory O'Reilly, Administrator, St Francis Medical Centre Mullingar; Mrs Leona Walsh, secretary to Dr Moore-Groarke and to the many anonymous patients who allowed us to use their case histories.

# ACKNOWLEDGEMENTS

# PREFACE

If you have gone to the trouble of buying this book, or borrowing it, or are interested enough to take it off the shelf and open it, then the chances are you or someone close to you has a problem. But take heart – you are not alone – as you will see as you peruse the pages that follow; and furthermore you, or the person you want to help, *can get better*. You have just taken the first step. The journey is neither easy nor is it quick, but it is possible. I know – I have made it.

So read on, take hope and good luck.

*Jenny Seagrove*

# INTRODUCTION

In the last ten years many treatment centres for eating disorders have been set up throughout the country. To date no register exists as to the exact percentage of Irish people suffering from *anorexia nervosa*, *bulimia nervosa* and *compulsive eating disorders*. Some studies estimate that approximately one in five Irish people between the ages of 15 and 30 will suffer from an eating disorder at some stage in their lives. Some of these individuals will make a spontaneous recovery from their disorder but others will require intensive in-patient and out-patient treatment programmes.

Many people who suffer from eating disorders never look for professional help. These sufferers must not be forgotten. Over the four years that Dr Moore-Groarke has been working in the area of eating disorders, she and her colleagues have received numerous letters and telephone enquiries from sufferers who never find the courage to take that first step and make an appointment. Often it is only when sufferers become medically at risk that they seek professional help. This is usually at an accident and emergency ward of a general hospital following a drug overdose that is really a desperate plea for help.

The Health Promotion Unit in this country has produced some very useful information on healthy eating but has not as yet produced a preventative programme on eating disorders to be used in schools. Much of the work of the staff of St Francis Medical Centre involves going around to schools and educating teenagers about the severe consequences of such eating disorders. Usually, we are accompanied by some of our patients in this exercise.

Thankfully, eating disorders are now treated much more seriously among members of the medical profession than in the past. They realise that their role lies in medically monitoring and, in severe cases, stabilising a patient's physical health. Medical practitioners also realise the importance of psychological intervention in helping the sufferer move towards recovery. We think this is true for medical personnel not just in cases of eating disorders but for any addiction. The GP is often the first link in the chain of a multi-disciplinary approach to treatment.

In the case of obese patients, the medical profession plays a vital role in assessing possible organic causes for the condition. Because there is often a high degree of manipulation and denial on the part of patients, sometimes (albeit rarely), a patient is misdiagnosed (e.g. as having irritable bowel syndrome, Crohn's disease, etc.) but for the most part it is the patient who usually convinces the doctor that he or she could not possibly have an eating disorder. Many individuals will reject the doctor's diagnosis and consult other consultants to disprove the diagnosis. Often this viewpoint is also held by the family members, thus reinforcing the sufferer's denial.

This is the first Irish book that looks at all three eating disorders. It will help to clarify issues for family and friends of sufferers. It presents the facts regarding the complexities of accepting, treating and recovering from eating disorders. It also deals with moments of despair which result for patients and family when a patient goes into relapse.

It presents real life case histories (which have been disguised somewhat for reasons of confidentiality) many of which are from male sufferers in an attempt to dispel the myth that eating disorders are just a female disorder. The honesty and openness of the patients who describe their experiences for the book is to be admired and we thank them sincerely. Much of what we know about eating disorders we have learned from sufferers. They have placed their trust in us and in turn we hope that we have helped to make life easier for them.

Patients have been wonderful in supporting us as professionals in our mission to increase public awareness of eating disorders. They have gone on radio and television and accompanied us on many school talks and described how food became their enemy. Several public figures (such as Britt Ekland and Jenny Seagrove) have also spoken of their battle with eating disorders.

The publication of Andrew Morton's book, *Diana, Her Own Story,* did much to publicise the whole area of eating disorders throughout the world. Sadly, for Karen Carpenter, her anorexia nervosa killed her. This book also shows that certain subgroups of individuals such as athletes are more prone to eating disorders and gives practical advice to coaches on how to deal with sufferers.

We hope that this book will help make eating disorders a little more comprehensible and perhaps a little less frightening than they might otherwise seem. Food need not become your enemy.

GILLIAN MOORE-GROARKE
SYLVIA THOMPSON

# 1

# EATING DISORDERS – A FEMALE DISEASE?

*A western disease – how our way of life and the ideals of western society make some people hate their bodies.*

The word anorexia generally conjures up memories from teenage years of a friend in a group of classmates who became obsessed with dieting to a dangerous extent. Most of us can remember hazy incidents at school when one of the girls (it was usually a girl although this is changing) had to take time off because she had become so thin and depressed that she could no longer concentrate in class. Although we didn't always know exactly what was happening to her, anorexia was the catch-all word that explained away her problem.

Unfortunately, extreme dieting and concerns about weight and shape are so widespread in our society that they are now perceived to be normal. Thinness is associated with positive attributes such as intelligence, beauty, greater attractiveness, youth, health and personal as well as professional power so it is not surprising that every teenager wants to be thin.

While thinness is rewarded by western cultures, fatness is punished. We are all aware of the jokes about people who are overweight. Although they may not appear harmful, research has shown that negative jokes and comments about fat people are part of an underlying prejudice against being fat.

Stereotypes of fat people include other characteristics such as laziness, ugliness, dirtiness or even stupidity. Such prejudices creep into the home and workplace making life on the whole much more difficult for any individual who is overweight and even for those who don't fit the narrow definition of thinness.

Although it is almost impossible to calculate the effect that the two-fold message of reward for thinness and punishment for fatness has on the individual, most people perceive themselves to be fatter than they are and therefore desire to be thinner. The greater the discrepancy between the perceived self and the ideal self, the greater the desire for change and consequently increased dieting occurs.

Approximately 70% of women in western cultures between the ages of 25 and 54 will admit to being on a diet at some stage of their lives. Women report a greater body dissatisfaction than men although dissatisfaction among the male population is steadily increasing. On a deeper level, body dissatisfaction is usually associated with low self-esteem and this is true for women as well as men.

Body dissatisfaction can vary from a mild dislike of the body's appearance to an intense hatred of it, and teenagers are in the high-risk category when it comes to having a negative body image.

Such negative body feelings draw people into a web of food preoccupation and puts a huge emphasis on the food we eat: when and how often we eat, and what we eat. Most people are now aware of the nutritional value and the calorific content of their food and generally speaking try to balance diets in terms of protein, fat, carbohydrate and fibre content.

However, the danger lies in an obsessive desire to control the exact amount of calorific intake – especially when that amount is below our normal daily requirements. When people become too focused on how fattening certain foods are and how important it is to avoid them they may be on the way to developing a serious problem with food.

The fact that health professionals increasingly stress the importance of diet and exercise is in itself a positive development in our society. However, like all good things, its positive message can be abused. The number of gymnasiums and health centres is continuing to rise and the danger of over-exercise is as big a problem as the abuse of food. The characteristic health-consciousness of the 1990s leads to the search for the perfect body which can allow anorexics hide their food and fitness obsessions behind a fashionable image.

The dangers of this perfect-body pursuit are highlighted by models, dancers and athletes, when they talk about the difficulties of their profession. Their bodies often carry the physical damage caused by years of self-starvation. English model, Celia Hammon, once said, 'If I had been left to my own devices, I would have died of starvation by now.' And Beverly Johnson, a colleague of Celia, admitted to having developed a thyroid problem because of years of crash diets. 'One day my mother dragged me out of the shower and stood me in front of a three-way mirror, and I looked like a Biafran. I started to cry but it didn't stop me dieting. I think I will always have an eating disorder now.'

A perfect-body image can also affect gay men in that their real selves may always appear a long way off from their ideals. The thin but muscular gay stereotype is as desirable for gay men as the size ten model is for women.

One in ten people now seeking help for an eating disorder in this country is male and those most at risk of developing a problem are male models, dancers, athletes and gays because body image is such an important part of their identity.

Eating disorders can be divided into three main categories – anorexia, bulimia and obesity. All three conditions are more common in females than males. Health professionals believe that eating disorders in general are the fastest growing neuroses in the western world.

ANOREXIA NERVOSA put simply is undereating to the point of starvation. It is characterised by a preoccupation with body weight and food, weight loss, an intense fear of gaining weight, a distorted body image and the cessation of monthly menstruation among female sufferers.

The onset of symptoms is likely to occur at times of stress (when parents split up, when the individual is changing schools, when someone close to her dies). Anorexics tend to isolate themselves, withdrawing from all social contacts while at the same time becoming perfectionist in the food obsessed world they create. They are unhappy, lonely and confused while they continue to starve themselves. They need help.

BULIMIA NERVOSA is characterised by repeated episodes of compulsive binge-eating with or without self-induced vomiting and/or laxative abuse. People with bulimia can be normal, under- or overweight and they often hide their problem by appearing cheerful and relaxed.

Bulimics generally overeat in private, consuming vast amounts of high calorie food until their stomachs ache. Self-induced vomiting can provide a temporary relief but they move into a cycle of overeating followed by vomiting or laxative abuse which leads to a feeling of total hopelessness.

It is an expensive habit – as much as £40 worth of food can be eaten at one binge. This sometimes leads to further problems such as shoplifting, or lying and cheating to justify the money spent. In most cases, the binge/purge cycle is an outlet for feelings of frustration, disappointment, anger, loneliness and boredom.

Although bulimics are more willing to seek help to find relief from their problem, psychologists have found that at least 40% of anorexics also suffer from bulimia.


OBESITY is the excessive accumulation of fat in the body. People who are 20% above the average weight for their age, height and sex are said to be obese. Obesity tends to run in families, as some people follow their parents' habits and become 'comfort' eaters. However, it can in some instances be caused by inherited medical complications.

Obesity is most common in only children and often more likely to occur in the youngest child. The marked decrease in physical activity in affluent societies seems to be a major factor in the recent rise in obesity as a public health problem.

Although obese people tend to have lower levels of anxiety and depression than the general population, they have to endure the negative stereo-type associated with being fat.

### Male Patient's Personal Experience

Jack was 27 when he first attended as an out-patient. He started having chest pains, and a blood test revealed low potassium levels. During a visit to his GP, he happened to mention that he had also had numerous visits to his dentist for erosion of tooth enamel. It was his GP's perception that led Jack to come out and admit his bulimia:

'I used to be nicknamed "Fatso" by my rugby team-mates. I remember one day after a school match when I was thirteen, I could make myself sick by sticking my finger at the back of my throat. After that, I would make myself sick every day, sometimes after every time I ate. I began to feel happy that I had found a way to make myself thin-ner and more attractive. After all, I didn't want to be the only team member without a girlfriend as I got older.

'Over the years, I also became addicted to pre-scribed medication which was supposed to help with my depression. I hated myself so much. In the space of any one year my weight used to fluctuate by as much as three-quarters of a stone. Even now although I am doing OK in my career, when I am under stress, I can't wait to leave for home and binge for two to three hours on anything I can lay my hands on. I just can't stop.

'I left home because I was afraid my parents would find out and I think that my sister suspected something was wrong. It is a very lonely illness. I could never tell any of the lads even though I once saw another team-mate getting sick after a game, just like me.

'I regret not saying anything before now. It was only when my girlfriend discovered what I was doing that I went for help. I suppose I didn't think it was the manly thing to do.'

Jack's progress is still quite slow. He is now one year down the road and still has occasional lapses usually associated with periods of stress at work. He has had to examine his family structure where being the best at sport took precedence over everything else. He remembers his father pushing him to get fit, get on the rugby team and his whole life would fall into place. He knew deep down he would never be as good a player as his older brother was and this feeling of inferiority was coped with alone by becoming bulimic.

# 2

# TELL-TALE SIGNS

*How to be sure that a friend or family member has an
eating problem*

Perhaps you know somebody who suffers from an eating disorder and you are worried. Maybe you are just suspicious and you don't know where to go to find out if your suspicions are justifiable. The sufferer may be your child, a friend or even your spouse.

Regardless of what age the individual is, it is important to remember that anorexia, bulimia and obesity are outward signs of something that is seriously wrong inside. The problem is really related to a personal identity crisis of some sort.

Eating disorders provide a way of trying to reach a position of independence or control when the struggle towards self-identity proves difficult or a comfortable self-image becomes almost unobtainable. Taking control of the body and food intake can strangely be the only way of achieving any control in the life of the sufferer. As a parent or someone close to the sufferer, you can be both helpful and harmful in understanding this struggle. Either way, it will not be easy for you.

In this chapter, we will give you a list of the warning signs of anorexia, bulimia and obesity starting with the more obvious behavioural indications and finishing with the medical signs which come into focus when the condition has reached a dangerous level.

### *Warning Signs – Anorexia Nervosa*

• Making excuses for not eating such as: 'I've eaten at a friend's house' or 'I'll cook something later for myself'.

• Peculiar way of handling food such as breaking it up into little pieces and not eating it at all.

• An obsessive interest in food to the extent of cooking meals for all the family and then avoiding eating.

• A sudden avoidance of foods containing animal fats or becoming vegetarian.

• Denial of hunger or that there is a problem with eating.

• Wearing baggy clothes to hide 'thinness'.

• Social withdrawal and mood swings – friends stop ringing and sufferers avoid going out. They become irritable and agitated.

• Fear of gaining weight and/or a destructive desire to continue losing weight. Clients start off losing a few pounds and their target weight becomes lower and lower. The anorexic shows an abnormal weight loss of 10 per cent or more with no known medical evidence accounting for the loss.

• Sufferer weighs him/herself numerous times a day in many cases after every meal. Anorexics often become frantic if they do not have access to a weighing scales. They also have a distorted body image in that when they look at themselves in the mirror, they see themselves twice or three times their actual size.

• Traces of vomit in the toilet or in bins in the bedroom or study are often a frightening sign that someone in the house is vomiting, using diuretics and/or laxatives to lose weight.

• The anorexic becomes perfectionist about everything he/she does usually ending up dissatisfied with most things.

Medical warning signs associated with anorexia include symptoms of starvation such as dry or flaky skin and lanugo (fine body hair) growing on the body. The hands and feet can become mothly blue because of poor circulation and ankles and feet swell due to a shortage of protein.

Female anorexics tend to lose their monthly periods because their bodies can no longer sustain normal bodily functions and psychosomatic loss of taste and smell occurs in a small number of cases.

Low blood pressure and a slow heart pulse can in very serious cases lead to heart failure.

### *Case History of an Anorexic*
#### (As told by her mother)

'Jean left in October to go to university. She moved into digs – since she didn't know anybody else going to the same university, her father and I felt this was the best option. She returned home in December for the Christmas break looking very tired and thin. She was always very slight but she now looked terribly gaunt and pale. She refused to go to our local doctor and said that her course was very difficult, that she was under a lot of pressure and her landlady was cooking food she didn't like.

'She requested a change of accommodation and we agreed that she could change digs the following term, which she did. Six weeks later, she rang us to say she was feeling awful and wanted to come home for a break. In that six weeks she had lost more weight. She was refusing to eat with us and when on the rare occasion, she did, she always insisted on serving her own portions. When we went into the bathroom, I noticed the bathroom scales had been moved. She didn't want to return to college but we insisted until she told us what was wrong.

'At Easter break, Jean agreed to go to see a

doctor who ruled out any medical evidence for weight loss. He referred her to a psychiatrist who diagnosed her as having anorexia. We were both shocked and found this hard to believe. She had gone from being a happy-go-lucky child to a very aggressive and withdrawn person. When we spoke to the psychiatrist, he told us her main difficulty was in moving away from home and that she could not accept that life went on as normal while she was away at college. Her older sister moved out because each time Jean came home, the two of them were constantly arguing.

'Jean eventually went into hospital and spent five months in an in-patient programme. As a family, we also went into therapy and we took all the blame upon ourselves. We couldn't accept where we had gone wrong. My husband and I started arguing and our ten year old son was totally confused at the change in his family environment. Jean was manipulating us all in an attempt to gain "all of" our affections. It took a long time for her to reach some level of stability and we all had to make some necessary changes.'

Jean's story is an example of how anorexic sufferers are discovered. When Jean's mother later rang up her two landladies, she found out that Jean had not been eating and was making no attempt to make friends with the other students living in the house.

## *Warning Signs – Bulimia Nervosa*

• Bulimic sufferers exhibit a fear of gaining weight and dissatisfaction with their body weight and shape. They often ask questions like: 'Do I look fat in these jeans? etc.' and they can spend hours in the bathroom in front of the mirror. Bulimics often go on low calorie diets or attend weight-loss classes.

• Prolonged exercise for the purpose of weight control. For example a bulimic sufferer may do 50 lengths of the swimming pool, followed by 30 minutes jogging.

• Bulimics are usually within 15 pounds of their normal body weight so they do not look as emaciated as anorexic sufferers. Their weight does, however, fluctuate because of constant bingeing and purging. It is secretive binge-eating followed by attempts to purge the food through self-induced vomiting which is the primary activity of bulimic sufferers.

• Bulimics are often moody and depressive although they appear to be happy and cheerful. They tend to become unsociable because they feel nobody understands them and also the financial debts they incur from bingeing inhibit their social life. They can be very moody especially if access to the bathroom is difficult or, wanting to binge, other people's presence in the house prevents them from doing so.

- Bulimic sufferers often have black teeth from the hydrochloric acid in the stomach brought up by constant vomiting.

Medical warning signs of bulimia include problems with the throat, oesophagus, stomach and colon due to constant vomiting and swollen salivary glands in the neck. A lack of potassium because of inadequate diet can lead to cardiac problems, and loss of energy can bring on muscle weakness and nervous tension. Female bulimics also suffer from menstrual irregularities.

### *Female Bulimic's Personal Story*

Sharon was caught shoplifting for the second time. The first time she had been let off with a caution but this time she was taken to court and her 'secret' was now out in the open. What made it worse was that as a trainee solicitor, she now felt everybody would despise her.

She came for help with tremendous motivation. She had started making herself sick when she first left home at the age of 21 following the break-up of a relationship which had lasted two years:

'I felt such a hypocrite. To the world, I was a successful, outgoing girl. I was the life and soul of the party. People were amazed at my will-power and ability to eat and drink sensibly. They never

noticed my relatively long lapses in eating. I somehow managed to disguise them.

'Inside I felt rotten to the core. It was like I was
leading two different lives – one for the world at
large who all thought I was coping so well after my
break-up with Mark. Little did they know that my
other hidden world was "my world of food". As
long as I looked okay to the world, then it didn't
matter so much. My performance at work remained
the same and I felt so proud anytime anyone said I
had lost weight.

'I now know that I had no independence. I
couldn't survive alone and when Mark left me, my
world fell apart. But as my bulimia progressed, I
became more miserable and more filled with self-
hatred, desperation and terrible guilt. It was not
easy. After all I had portrayed such a perfect image.
Deep inside I felt so rejected. I was getting more
and more into debt as I was still buying clothes and
other things as well as spending a small fortune on
food. I had exceeded my limit on all three credit
cards and that is when I started shoplifting and
thought I would never get caught. What a fool I
was!'

Sharon has since returned to her legal career and is
now in a new relationship. What she had to realise
was that her own insecurity and lack of independence led her – from the age of 16 – never to being

without a boyfriend. Mark was the first man to walk out of her life. She tried to control him and when she didn't succeed he left. Her world fell apart and it took her all of eighteen months to realise that her behaviour was not normal.

## *Similarities between Anorexia Nervosa and Bulimia Nervosa*

- Preoccupation with dieting, food, weight and body size.
- Discomfort when eating with other people.
- Noticeable changes in habits, mood and personality.
- Hyperactive behaviour, inability to relax, difficulty in concentrating and poor sleeping patterns.
- Complaints about tiredness, headaches, unexplained swelling of the glands and muscle weakness.
- Constant search for approval by sufferers for looks, clothes and anything they do around the house.
- Problems with interpersonal relationships, feeling by sufferers that everybody is against them and that nobody understands how they feel.

## Differences between Anorexia Nervosa and Bulimia Nervosa

• Anorexic patients deny their abnormal eating behaviour while bulimics recognise that bingeing and purging is not normal.

• The anorexic tends to be introverted while the bulimic appears to be extroverted.

• The anorexic turns away from food in order to cope while the bulimic, like the comfort eater, uses food as a coping device. The anorexic has a distorted body image while the bulimic expresses dissatisfaction with body weight and shape.

• The anorexic has a preoccupation with continuing to lose more and more weight while the bulimic has a pre-occupation with attaining an ideal if not a realistic normal weight.

## Warning Signs of Compulsive Overeating

Obesity is usually the easiest of all eating disorders to detect because of the obvious physical changes. However, parents often tend to ignore their teenagers gaining of weight, putting it down to 'puppy fat'. This often encourages the sufferer to continue eating too much.

• There is a history of obesity in your family and you notice that your child is putting on weight.

• The individual has no interest in sports or

exercise of any sort and is becoming a 'couch potato'.

• The person in question has a poor self-image, lacks confidence and has few friends.

• Mood swings, aggressive outbursts at being denied certain foods.

• Unsuccessful dieting, secretive eating, spending pocket money on sweets or eating a lot of junk food.

• The person denies being overweight or admits he/she feels guilty about being overweight.

• The client overeats in association with stressful life events, for example exams or (if a female sufferer) she puts all her overeating down to pre-menstrual tension.

• The client avoids family or social gatherings because of weight.

• The child says that he/she is bullied at school or called names for being fat.

Medical complications associated with obesity include diabetes, gall-bladder disease, high blood pressure, cancer of the breast or colon, heart and/or respiratory failure and osteoarthritis.

Obese people may also have complications at surgery since they require higher doses of anaesthetic during an operation and the surgeon has to cut through more than normal fat which leads to larger scars and greater proneness to post-operative infection.

## Female Patient's Personal Experience

Jeanette was overweight for as long as she could remember. She was an only child and when she first came to therapy, she described her belief that the only way her parents ever showed her love was by feeding her. She had graduated from her course at college and had been unemployed for nine months. She felt her weight was preventing her from gaining employment and it was then she decided to take the initiative and seek professional help.

'I was always trying to control my weight and all my life was continually on a diet. I kept trying but never got anywhere. I'd start every Monday with such enthusiasm and if I was extremely lucky, I'd last until Tuesday evening. By Tuesday evening, I'd go out and buy four or five bars of chocolate. Once again, I was on the "pig's back". I was on the roller coaster and had no desire to get off until the next time I'd overhear somebody saying, "How could she let herself go like that!" To the outside world, I ate less than everybody else but most of my eating was done in secret; I would eat alone in my bedroom.

'During my adolescence I succeeded four times in losing large amounts of weight. I looked and felt great then I'd get too cosy and slacken off my restrictions. I'd find I had put on a few pounds and I'd think what the heck, what's a few pounds? The next thing was that I was back on the merry-go-round of overeating and putting on more weight.

'A really good friend knew how I felt. She knew that I was continuously making excuses to avoid social occasions. I hated the way I looked, not being able to get clothes to fit, feeling uncomfortable in the theatre or at the cinema. My friend told me that she felt I could not lose weight on my own and needed some help.

'At about that time, my father fell ill and I began gaining more and more weight. It was only then that I realised that I was concealing my true feelings behind my weight.'

When Jeanette came for help she soon learned to control food and not to allow food control her. Her fear of losing her father following his heart attack led her to confront her inability to talk about her feelings. Because she was ten stone overweight, she also had to realise that it would be a slow process towards recovery, and that anything she learned this time, would mean lifelong changes.

*Athletes with Eating Disorders:*
*Warning Signs*

In the fitness/sport population, between 15% and

30% of young women and up to 5% of young men are suffering from an eating disorder. Tragically some of the best and brightest young participants are the most likely to be affected. The addictive behaviour becomes compulsive and uncontrolled, with disastrous, sometimes even fatal consequences. If an athlete seems to exhibit signs of an eating disorder, the following recommendations are in order:

### *How the Coach or Instructor Can Help*

- Arrange a private meeting with the athlete.
- Ensure the meeting is supportive and not threatening.
- Listen to the athlete, and indicate your suspicions.
- Confirm that an admission of addiction need not necessarily jeopardise team participation.
- Assess whether professional intervention is necessary.
- Reassure the athlete that he/she need not be regarded as a failure if confirmation of your suspicions is given.
- Arrange for follow-up meetings whether or not the athlete agrees to seek help at that particular time.
- Confirm with the athlete how important his/her role in sport is to them.

## Other Points to Notice

- It is not advisable to question team-mates instead of talking directly to the athlete.
- Disciplining the athlete will destroy any rapport that exists.
- Indicate to the athlete that you know 'what is going on' rather than report specific reasons which lead to your suspicions.
- Make the athlete aware that you will be checking back.
- Disassociate yourself from any personal developmental issues of the problem.
- Ensure confidentiality among other team members.

### Case History of an Athlete Suffering from Bulimia

Rita was 16 years old and suffering from bulimia. For four years she had been training hard to join a team as a gymnast. Following an accident in which she broke both her legs, she started to gain weight. She spent three months in a wheelchair and had to learn to walk again. She was devastated when she was told that she could not return to gymnastics. She felt such a failure and felt she had let down her coach and her team-mates. She could not cope with the fact that she was so quickly replaced on the team or begin to understand how it happened. As soon as she recognised that she had gained weight, she started to make herself sick. Within weeks she was sticking her fingers in the back of her throat every time she ate to make herself sick. She became socially withdrawn and started to hate herself. She refused to go out. Her family described her as having a split personality. Her school grades were dropping and she had difficulty in concentrating for even the shortest periods of time.

Finally, it got too much for her and she confided in her mother who went to great lengths to get help for her. Rita had to start believing in herself again; she had to stop pushing her body beyond its capabilities. Slowly she began to realise that the accident was not her fault and she had other creative talents that she could now focus on.

### Dos and Don'ts when Living with a Sufferer of an Eating Disorder

Do
- Learn all you can about the eating disorder.
- Discuss with the sufferer his/her feelings and problems with openness and acceptance.
- Ask the sufferer how you can help.
- Encourage him/her to take responsibility for the condition.
- Continue to listen.
- Be patient; don't expect change overnight. Re-

covery can be a long slow process.

- Watch for health-threatening physical or emotional symptoms.
- Refuse to be caught up in arguments and battles regarding food.
- Emphasise positive characteristics rather than appearance.
- Offer physical affection, even if it is shrugged off.
- Explain what is wrong to the other children in the family.
- Seek early professional treatment, even if the sufferer refuses help. You will benefit from going for counselling yourself.

**Don't**
- Try to force-feed the sufferer or to deprive the over-eater.
- Weigh him/her or insist on loss or gain in weight.
- Discuss food or reinforce his/her preoccupation with food instead of feelings.
- Treat him/her like a helpless child.
- Tell him/her that he/she is nauseating, gross, disgusting.
- Make a moral issue out of it, e.g., saying, 'Think of all the children in famine countries'.
- Be neurotic about your own appearance or eating.

- Compare him/her to other siblings/peers.
- Allow the sufferer to control or upset the entire family.
- Place blame on yourself or others.

The most important thing in trying to help the sufferer is to try to continue living your own life as normally as possible. Don't let illness rule your life too. Look after your own needs and desires. You are entitled to your own feelings. If you are to encourage the sufferer to express feelings openly and honestly you must set an example.

Accept that the character changes are part of the illness. The sufferer may become deceitful or even start shoplifting, as we mentioned in the last chapter. He/she needs help rather than judgement. Progress tends to create difficulties between parents and sufferer because it will involve a more assertive attitude and a degree of separation. This will be a struggle for all of you. You may feel that you, as well as the sufferer, need some counselling about your own feelings. Don't be afraid to ask. Progress requires change.

The men in the family should realise that the sufferer and the rest of the family need their help. Don't opt out by regarding this as women's work. Try to share your feelings and ideas, your work and leisure with the rest of the family. Accept them as equals and respect their views so that they feel happy sharing their fears, concerns and experiences with you as well.

# 3

# THE FAMILY AND ITS INFLUENCE

Parents of anorexic or bulimic sufferers often feel that the home has become a battleground where food is used as a weapon or a powerful means of control. Many conflicting messages pass between the sufferer and the parents. For example, it is very common to hear: 'Leave me alone or I will not eat anything'; 'Let me live my own life; I'll eat what I want', or more upsetting still: 'Don't ever leave me or I'll stop eating altogether.'

The contradictory feelings thus generated are very difficult to live with for all the family but it is, however, important that they come out in the open. If you have a child with an eating disorder, you will probably feel totally helpless and very worried. You may even wonder if you are to blame.

When the home environment becomes very tense, parents also lose control of their feelings and move between really wanting to help their child and deeply resenting the existence of a problem that has upset the entire family. It is quite common for parents in therapy to say things like: 'I'd do anything to make him better', or 'I can't bear to see her so unhappy', and 'She is ruining our lives', or 'At times, I despise him for this'. Some parents of anorexic sufferers go as far as denying the plain fact that their child is underweight in an attempt to hide their sense of shame.

## What Often Happens

Some sufferers act as a liaison for parents whose marriage is going through a difficult time. The anorexic is then blamed as the cause of all current family problems. In such families there is also a tendency for each member of the family to speak not for himself or herself but in someone else's name, always modifying, correcting or invalidating what the other person has said. (For example when the father comes home drunk and the mother confronts him, the anorexic may take either of their sides.) This type of communication is often a desperate attempt (by the anorexic or a brother or sister) to uncover a deeper problem which one member of the family (often a parent) continuously refuses to admit.

Studies show that some anorexic and bulimic sufferers have been the victims of sexual abuse by a family member. Instead of admitting this experience to themselves, they grow to hate their bodies and themselves. In such cases starvation or bingeing and purging becomes a way of punishing themselves while keeping the abuse a secret even to themselves for a long period of time.

Understanding fully what is going on within the family is the key to the problem because in many cases the child's eating disorder is a direct result of an underlying family problem which is not being adequately dealt with. In a way, the child has become the 'symptom bearer' of the problem. Such a problem is revealed when the child gets a chance to express with complete honesty why he or she became so desperate as to become anorexic or bulimic. Generally speaking, obesity does not happen as a result of unhealthy family dynamics but more often because of lifestyle problems which the child may inherit from either parent. We will deal with this later in the chapter.

Often families of eating disorder sufferers seem to the outsider to be very close, with every family member intensely involved with the others. Quite often this over-protectiveness lies at the root of the eating disorder because it is hiding some deeper more painful vulnerability. It is this 'family secret' which has to be revealed for the sufferer to get well again and for the family to move on from the episode intact.

A failure to achieve a sense of independence from the family is characteristic of all anorexics. They are often afraid of being criticised and are not certain of their parent's love. These parents tend to present their family life as more harmonious than it actually is or they deny difficulties altogether. Usually there is very little physical affection shown in anorexic families.

Many bulimic patients admit to feeling unusually strong family ties and psychologists believe that this does in fact disrupt the child's self-development. In therapy, bulimics have over-protective parents, particularly mothers, and their self-starvation reflects an effort to assert and separate themselves from maternal intrusion while the bingeing is an attempt to compensate for the loneliness they feel from the lack of affection from a mother (who is often cold and aloof in spite of being over-protective).

Fears of growing up and becoming separate from the family is a common contributing factor to eating disorders. Teenagers often feel vulnerable about leaving home, starting relationships and getting (or not getting) a job. Some parents simply don't have the confidence themselves to encourage their children to face these challenges of growing-up. Sometimes they project their own inadequacies onto their children who then develop great fears about their future which find expression in anorexia or bulimia.

For example, when Jackie went to a prestigious boarding school, she not only suffered from leaving home but she also felt a failure when she experienced academic difficulties. Until that time she had been convinced that she was the 'perfect daughter of perfect parents'. She wanted to be a child again. She became bulimic because she wanted to be her parents 'little girl'. Like many bulimics, she didn't want to grow up.

Parents of anorexics and bulimics are often perfectionists, expecting high performance from their children in all aspects of their lives. Sometimes the desire for children to be good at sports, have lots of friends and do exceptionally well in their exams is rooted in parents' sense of failure in their own lives. And in fact, many parents have admitted in family therapy that they were trying to relive their own lives. It is only when the child develops anorexia or bulimia (as an expression of their failure to reach parental expectations) that some parents realise the unfair pressure they have been exerting.

Other parents have mixed feelings themselves about their child leaving home. Their uncertainties may be associated with a fear of facing new situations. For example in a marriage where communication is bad, a mother may unconsciously overprotect her child from the world to avoid having to confront her own unhealthy relationship with her husband.

In the families of some anorexics, the mother

may appear to behave in a very childish way towards her husband and the female anorexic patient then mirrors this behaviour in an attempt to gain the father's attention and affection.

## WHEN THE FAMILY DYNAMIC IS WRONG
### *Bernadette's experience*

Bernadette grew up on a farm and was a happy and healthy child until she reached her teens. She was of average build and an early maturer. After some teasing at school about being too chubby, she suddenly decided to lose weight. She avoided any activities with her friends because she felt huge. She began to believe that they did not like her. In five months she lost half her body weight and her periods stopped.

During family therapy, the focus was on why Bernadette went to such extremes to gain attention? As a child, she was very close to her father but as she got older she regressed to a clinging relationship with her mother. They lived with her grandparents who still owned the farm. Bernadette's grandmother complained that her father was spending too much time with her and was ignoring everybody else.

During therapy Bernadette had to regain a position of respect in the family. As a result of her mother's therapy, her parents' relationship also improved because she always felt Bernadette's father was closer to his own mother than to her. For family therapy to be successful, the family members as well as the patient have to be well-motivated and willing to be honest about their feelings. They must also be prepared to change the way they behave if it is found to be inappropriate.

Some parents reject treatment for themselves because they feel if they admit such a need, it implies that their rearing of their child was faulty in some way. Usually, those who reject therapy in such a context are the families that have serious emotional problems. Often the mothers show a nearly uncontrollable anger about the illness.

One such case concerned Brian whose mother believed that his anorexia exposed her to his friends as an incompetent parent. His father also believed that his wife's needs came first. Brian was constantly criticised for the way he dressed and during most family arguments he was attacked for being too like his friends: too selfish, too arrogant and not cultured enough. His mother essentially wanted to control his life. When away from home during college term, his anorexia wasn't as severe.

In therapy, it became obvious that if Brian didn't eat, his mother saw it as a rejection of her. His parents wanted to change him back to the young pleasing child that he once was. It took them a long time to accept that Brian had grown up and was fighting for his freedom by 'controlling his eating habits'.

The onset of puberty with its striking changes in physique and behaviour can threaten sexually inhibited parents and marriages where sexuality has engendered one unhappy spouse. Young people who have learned from their parents – either through dismissive comments or embarrassed silences – that sex is unpleasant, may panic at the onset of bodily changes and growing sexual impulses.

Teenagers who have experienced sexual abuse will have further unexplainable fears which will encourage them either to be promiscuous at an early age or avoid sexual relationships completely. In either case, anorexia or bulimia can become a way of avoiding having to deal with such emotions while sending out a message that all is not well.

### Case History from a Bulimic's Parent

Here a father describes how he came to discover his daughter's bulimia. As a lone parent, this was very difficult for him to cope with especially since his wife had died eighteen months earlier.

'My daughter Tina is the eldest of three girls. My wife died of breast cancer some months ago. I was away from home a lot as my job as a representative took me all over the country. I relied on Tina to look after things and at first she seemed more than happy to oblige. She was always a great girl to help and had been particularly good when my wife had first become ill.

'I trusted Tina so much that I gave her money to buy the groceries and pay the bills but for the last four months, each time I came home at weekends, there was no food in the house and a lot of the bills were mounting up. I confronted Tina about this but I didn't get anywhere.

'Then one night some time later, I woke up about three in the morning as I thought I heard somebody getting sick. I got up to find Tina in the bathroom bringing up blood. When she discovered I was there, she broke down and told me the whole story: how she felt under so much pressure since her mother had died, how she felt she hadn't had time to grieve her mother's death and how she felt obliged to put on a brave face for all our sakes.

'I felt so guilty that I had taken her for granted that I broke down as well. I felt so insensitive, I had tried to impose my wife's role on my eldest daughter. I knew deep down something had to be done quickly or I would lose my daughter as well and I couldn't cope with a double loss. I also began to feel guilty about my other children: what would they think of me!

'I felt totally responsible for Tina's condition.

The next day, she went to our doctor who referred her to a psychologist. I agreed to go for bereavement counselling with the other girls and somehow I felt things would come right in the end.'

Things did come right in the end but not without difficult periods of change and adaptation. In a strange way, Tina's bulimia was a blessing in disguise because it gave all the family permission to confront their mother's death and not to ignore their grief.

## Obesity and the Family

Parents are the absolute role models for an obese child. Unhealthy eating habits and the use of food as a comfort device are practices often passed from parent to child. Families of overweight children are often lacking in physical affection and the parents who are all too aware of this try to compensate by 'feeding' the child. Many obese patients say things like: 'The only way my parents ever showed me love was by feeding me.'

There is a greater likelihood that the youngest child in a family will become obese as an indication of the parents' lack of ability to let go and recognise that their job is done. Over-protective mothers of only children also run the risk that their son/ daughter will become a food addict.

Many obese patients report that their parents

are obsessed with good image and weight control. They also admit during therapy that every time they defied their mother's attempts at controlling them, they were put on a diet.

## Case History of a Parent of an Obese Patient

Mark's mother describes how she noticed Mark gaining weight and the difficulty she had in trying to get him to confront the unpleasantness that he himself was creating.

'Mark was my only child. His father always had to be careful of his weight because of a family history of obesity and associated cardiac problems. Mark was always fond of his food and from the age of eleven, he started putting on weight. He refused to become involved in any of the school sports and when the other children in the estate were out playing, Mark was in front of the television or computer, or drawing in the study.

'When I refused to give him junk food, he became very aggressive and moody. He would say things like: "You don't love me", or "You don't want to make me happy", or "You are not my mother so don't tell me what to do". I would find all his trouser and jacket pockets full of sweet papers and on several occasions I would notice sweet food missing from the cupboard. It caused numerous arguments between my husband and because Mark was such a convincing liar I started to blame his father. I became quite depressed and blamed myself for what was going on because it was not by choice that Mark was an only child. I had nine miscarriages and was so grateful when we adopted Mark and at that age we were both too old to adopt another child.

'Communication between us deteriorated and Mark's teenage years were very difficult for everyone concerned. His father kept saying he would grow out of it but I could see Mark was shutting himself off more and more. While doing his leaving certificate, he expressed an interest in the air corps. It was only when the school guidance teacher told him that his weight would act as a prohibiting factor that he first thought about doing something about it.

'Mark was referred to a dietician but he didn't make any quick recovery. The dietician referred him to a psychologist because she believed that he was repressing emotional issues. It was only then that Mark made any progress and he started to lose weight in a healthy way. He joined a male support group and when he discovered that he wasn't alone, he knew he could then work on his problem.'

Mark had to work on his feelings of rejection of his natural parents. He also had a lot of guilt regarding his inability to communicate with his peers and blaming his adoptive parents. It was only during family therapy that all communication channels were re-opened.

In some cases of obesity it has been found that parents suffer from alcoholism or depression. Usually there is also rivalry with a sister or brother, and if a child feels that he/she is being compared unfavourably with another member of the family, food becomes a friend. A small number of people become obese because they are forced to take on a lot of responsibility at an early age, for example if a parent dies or if the father is having an affair and the mother uses the child as a confidant. Such a co-dependency between parent and child often leads to the child's turning to food as a source of comfort.

Throughout the world parenting courses are becoming more and more popular. While they are a great source of encouragement to parents, the truth is that there is no foolproof method when it comes to rearing children. This chapter shows how influenced we all are by our own origins and how in our attempt to give the best to our children, we can often end up being over-protective.

It is important to realise as parents that if our child is suffering from an eating disorder, the whole family needs to be examined. Do not be afraid to take a look at your own family and be honest with yourself about how things are dealt with. If you discover that your child has a problem, firstly look at your own situation and that of your partner, and consider how they may impinge on your child.

Often at times of hospital admissions, one or both parents feel left out and although they are relieved that their son/daughter or partner has started to eat again and is looking better, they feel let down by the fact that other people (the medical team) have managed to succeed where they failed. For effective therapy, the burden of responsibility should be shared between the family and the specialists in charge. In this way, full recovery can mean the child becomes reintegrated into the family without carrying blame for the problem for years to come.

### When Your Girlfriend/Boyfriend or Spouse has an Eating Disorder

Sometimes the person you are closest to is the most difficult person to talk to about a problem. This can certainly be the case if your partner develops an eating disorder. However, it is of utmost importance that as a husband, wife, boyfriend or girlfriend, you try to understand why your partner has gone to such extreme measures.

As in family situations, some older women resort to eating disorders as an escape from something they can't cope with in their lives. Perhaps your partner's relationship is beginning to remind her of that of her parents, something she most wanted to avoid. You must be prepared to be honest and supportive so that she can get to the root of the problem. Perhaps your very relationship is at the root of the problem and this needs to be faced. You may need psychological help yourself to come to terms with the issues that the eating disorder has forced to the surface.

# 4

# ADMITTING THE PROBLEM

Everyone who has an eating disorder experiences mixed feelings about recovery. While all anorexics say they want to recover, they also say that they do not want to put on any weight. Likewise, all bulimics and compulsive eaters would like to eat normally again, but first, they want to diet to lose their weight.

Once you start to admit that you have an eating disorder, you have to choose what, if anything, you are going to do about it. If you choose to try recovery, you have a long battle ahead of you and you will need as much support as you can get from your family and friends as well as from the professionals who will guide you through a treatment programme. The battle against an eating disorder is fought in the mind and you'll need all the help you can get, especially for those days when the negative feelings are strongest and you feel like giving up.

There is a strong feeling of surrender for many sufferers when they come to realise how important it is to share their feelings. Generally speaking, sufferers are unused to sharing their feelings with anyone – least of all a member of a medical team. Some sufferers try to push their eating problems and the underlying causes to the back of their minds, hoping that somehow they will miraculously disappear. The truth is this never happens. Bingeing will recur until the disorder has been properly dealt with and because very few sufferers are capable of dealing with the underlying cause of their problem (which deep down they recognise but are afraid to face up to), finding help is essential.

## The First Step Is Seeking Help

The first person you should contact when seeking help is your local general practitioner or family doctor. The doctor can thus assess the seriousness of the problem and refer the patient on to specialist help if necessary.

It may take a good deal of courage to go to or allow yourself to be taken to the family doctor about such a matter as a suspected eating disorder. It involves a kind of self-exposure which is usually painful and therefore tends to be avoided at all costs. Because of this patients often go to the doctor ostensibly with a more minor complaint (sore throat, chest pain, 'sleeping' problems) which allows the doctor to detect if there is something more serious going on.

Family doctors can also be difficult to talk to about such a sensitive issue, not only because they have usually known the patient since childhood but also because the sufferer may find it too embarrassing or upsetting to discuss sensitive family issues and other contributing factors of a very private nature.

However, that said, doctors today are very aware of disorders which have a psychological origin. Despite initial fears and concerns, patients usually find the GP to be much more accepting of the problem than they initially thought.

Having made an initial assessment, the doctor will decide what to do next. In some cases matters will be managed through regular check-ups at the surgery (with weekly weigh-ins) but more often than not, the patient is referred to a local specialist. The general practitioner will usually know of a local consultant, psychiatrist, psychologist or sometimes a physician who takes a special interest in eating disorders. Some patients are referred to a special dietary disorder unit for an initial assessment to determine what form of treatment (in-patient or out-patient) is more appropriate.

Treatment approaches should take the patient's whole being into consideration. As we have already discussed, the cause of eating disorders is often deep-rooted and closely linked to the individual's experience in the family. For this reason some form of psychotherapy should always be incorporated into the treatment of eating disorders and drug treatments used only in the short-term to alleviate physical symptoms.

It is also important that the patient plays an active role in the treatment process with the issue of food made less and less significant as the treatment evolves. The responsibility for healthy eating is slowly handed back to the patient. In her book, *The Art of Starvation*, Sheila McLeod is highly critical of strict regimes where the patients are confined to bed until they reach their 'target weight'. She makes the point that treatment must reinforce the need to live a normal adult life again, not make the patient feel punished for not conforming.

## *Becoming a Patient*

To become a patient is to put oneself in the care of a doctor or a medical team of psychologists, psychiatrists, counsellors, dieticians, occupational therapists, physiotherapists and nurses. It is very important that a good rapport is established between the patient and the professional from an early stage. The goal in the relationship should be one of partnership with a sense of equality, mutual trust and understanding.

Professionals have to be extremely careful to

avoid battles with patients because this will be viewed as an attempt to 'control' and their initial reaction will be to put up their defences. If this happens the patients tend to shelve their internal conflict and positive feelings about change which defeats the entire purpose of intervention.

Whatever treatment plan is agreed on, progress will usually be slow and sometimes not very smooth. However, as long as the patients have a good relationship with the medical team, there will always be hope and confidence in their ability to change. It is more useful to think of change as what the English psychiatrist, Palmer calls, 'a struggle giving way to personal growth', than it is to expect a 'cure'.

There is no guarantee as to how long the process of change will take as each patient must eventually find his/her own pace of recovery. However, the rewards of progress help even the most hopeless patients to overcome their negative feelings.

Here, Carol describes her relief at agreeing to treatment for her obesity because beforehand her life was miserable. Her self-esteem was so low that she was even afraid to go out.

'I became obese in my early teens. I was the younger of two girls and my older sister was Miss Perfect in my parents' eyes. They believed she could do nothing wrong. In contrast to her, I was a disgrace. I had to struggle to get reasonable grades in school and according to my parents, my choice of friends, the way I dressed and everything I did were appalling and unacceptable.

'I rebelled by eating my life away. I became more and more introverted and the more my parents criticised me, the more I ate and the more I refused to go out. I missed a lot of school by continually pretending to be ill. I thought to myself: now I'll give them something to talk about. I'll become that "fat slob" that they so insensitively called me time and time again (often in front of relatives and friends). I would hear them say things like: "What a pity, she would be nice looking if only she lost some weight!" How I hated them for their comments. They forcibly brought me to doctor after doctor but I was determined never to give in to them.

'It was only when my sister, Laura, failed her first year college exams that I felt she wasn't as perfect as they thought she was. I went to see a psychologist who actually listened to me. My God, to be listened to was such a great gift! I was so afraid of admitting that I had become powerless over food, that it took months of talking about my family before I really started to do anything about losing weight.

'It's funny, you know, that the feeling of losing weight is a far greater feeling than was the feeling of sedation every time I stuffed my face to blot out my pain. At first I felt I had surrendered in a battle I could have won but this was the first time I did something for myself. Of course, I was afraid, I tested the psychologist out over and over again but once I knew that I could trust her, I felt safe and admitted defeat.'

Many parents and family members who have been struggling for months with an anorexic, bulimic or obese teenager, have mixed feelings about their son/daughter going into treatment. This point has been made in the previous chapter, where we said that parents feel they have failed where 'complete outsiders' can succeed. It is important that patients are made aware of how their parents feel about this because often they too are saddened by the fact that their parents have 'abandoned' them to the professionals. In their confusion, parents often hand over complete responsibility for their child to the 'experts' yet at the same time, they bombard the medical team with questions like: 'How is she doing?' or 'What do you think is really wrong?'

While the professionals can assure patients that their parents are, in fact, very concerned about their progress, the parents must involve themselves as much as is necessary in the treatment. Some parents refuse blankly to become involved in family therapy and separate themselves further from their child by labelling their condition as 'madness'.

Often their fear of opening up deeper problems in the family is masked by anger and a refusal to understand what is really going on. The following story is that of Diarmuid whose parents were asked to participate in family therapy.

Diarmuid was five stone overweight and eighteen years old when he first came for treatment. He was a physical wreck. He agreed to an out-patient programme for weight management and was also closely monitored by his doctor. His father and mother always dropped Diarmuid at the clinic and returned one hour later to pick him up. They never rang to see what progress he was making. During one of the sessions, I asked Diarmuid how would he feel if I spoke to his parents, at which time he broke down crying. When I asked him why, he openly admitted: 'You know, doctor, they think I am mad and that is why I am coming to see you.' I was appalled at their inaccurate and insensitive assessment of the situation so I wrote to them. It was three months later when his father rang me in a state of anger, demanding to know why I wanted to see them. When I explained my reasons, he reluctantly agreed to attend an evening appointment when 'it would be dark and nobody would see him or his wife coming'. It took a long time to allay their fears of social stigma but eventually we did reach a breakthrough and Diarmuid is still attending for therapy today.

## Refusing to Go for Help

A major problem occurs when a sufferer persistently refuses to go for help. Such people are usually suffering both from poor physical health and deep psychological trauma yet they resist their own need for help. There is no easy answer to the question that parents so often ask professionals: 'How can I get my child to go for help?'

Before any professional treatment can be successful, the sufferer must accept the problem and have a desire to adapt to change or even to the suggestion of change. Most professionals, if they are completely honest with themselves, will admit that it is useless to try and encourage an unmotivated patient.

Whether the treatment is at an in-patient or out-patient level, those involved must realise that an eating disorder is similar to any other addiction in that the sufferer has first and foremost to acknowledge the destructive eating patterns and behaviour. However, unlike other addictions, a particular difficulty lies in the fact that we have to eat to live. So, a sufferer can not totally cut out the 'offending' behaviour but must make eating habits more normal.

It might seem best to confront the sufferer with the situation but again as we said earlier, to enter battle or to use scare tactics is usually inappropriate and ineffective. It is more useful to give the full details of the physical damage the condition will cause as this is what patients are more likely to listen to. Usually they are not fully aware of the physical effect of their illness and despite what they say, they do not want to die.

Sufferers will finally overcome their resistance to treatment if they recognise that the advantages clearly outweigh the disadvantages in taking a 'risk' and accepting treatment. Parents are often surprised when they are encouraged to give the sufferer space to make up his/her own mind but in our experience, compulsory intervention has never proved successful because coerced patients will only conform so that they can soon be released.

At St Francis Medical Centre, all our in-patients and out-patients agree to treatment voluntarily. We will never agree to committing a patient. When such an extreme intervention occurs, what in effect happens is that sufferers are granted a licence to continue their manipulative behaviour patterns.

In a lot of cases parents claim that once their child begins treatment, the problem seems to take over the lives of all the members of the family. Some parents also feel invaded by those treating the sufferer. However, it is important to stick with the treatment through all the difficult times as this is usually the only way that the problem can be dealt with permanently.

Group therapy can be a useful back-up support both to the sufferer and their families. A special group for parents/spouses/partners/siblings is organised at our clinic on a regular basis. Here, feelings are shared by all sufferers and the sense of isolation is overcome by the very fact of sharing the problem. Most sufferers are surprised at first to hear other members of the group express similar feelings and experiences to theirs. Some prefer only to listen in the beginning, gradually building up the courage to open up and share feelings that once seemed so awful that they were unbearable.

### One Person's Experience of Group Therapy

Margaret joined a group after eighteen months of one-to-one therapy. She describes her experience as follows:

'The first night I attended group, I was really frightened, I was so scared that I would be pounced on or forced to speak. I was welcomed into the group by all present and the ground rules of confidentiality, boundaries, etc., were all explained to me. For six weeks I just sat and listened. I felt all the others were so much stronger than I was; I also felt that they had progressed further than me. After a while I would identify with what the group members were saying. We did a lot of exercises using clay, collage, relaxation, etc. I soon found the courage to share my feelings, and once I took that risk or first step, I felt so much at ease. We exchanged phone numbers and if we have difficulties we ring each other from time to time. It is great to have support from people who know what you are going through.'

Group therapy should also be a part of follow-up treatment for sufferers, even though they may have completed individual and family therapy. It gives them the strength and motivation to continue the process of change. It is also useful in helping recovering anorexics or bulimics to overcome periods of vulnerability when they are under stress or simply feeling down.

The success of group therapy is based on the individual members' commitment and motivation to the group. Confidentiality is of utmost importance and it must be established right from the start. The group must be a safe place where patients feel they can readily take the risk of sharing their feelings. If this is the case patients will eventually feel that the group belongs to them and that they can receive a lot of benefit and support from it.

## Coping with Change

The anorexic has got to put on weight while the obese patient has got to try and lose weight. The bulimic has got to try and stop self-induced vomiting. Weight change is easy to measure but what is more difficult to monitor is attitude towards food and eating behaviour. This is why progress can be assessed only if honesty exists between the profess-ional and the patient.

The return of menstruation can make some female patients want to step backwards in terms of treatment. This is because they see the return of their periods as a signal of recovery which despite previous motivation, they find difficult to cope with.

Other patients realise that once they have changed their eating patterns and are making a 'good' recovery, they have lost their 'crutch'. Some-times, the old crutch is replaced with a new one in the form of excessive drinking or drug-taking. Since many eating disorder patients are cross-addicted, professionals must examine this possibil-ity at all stages of the treatment process. Such extra problems usually happen when the patients have not re-adjusted to the new changes in their lives or because there are certain secrets which they have failed to share in therapy.

The first genuine sign of recovery is that the in-dividuals can safely say that they can no longer re-turn to their old destructive patterns of behaviours. Patients who have seemingly been cured often re-turn for treatment later with a more serious form of the original problem. However, for most sufferers, the will to change will eventually come. Obviously the longer they have the condition, the greater the risk involved in letting go of it and learning how to adapt to change.

A word of advice for those who feel they may be developing an eating problem. Do not ever be afraid to admit the problem and seek help. Although it may take a while, you will eventually find a treatment programme that is appropriate for you. At the back of this book, you will find a list of organisations and individuals who specialise in the treatment of eating disorders in Ireland. A contact name and telephone number is provided should you feel the time is right to seek help but remember, it is always useful to contact your doctor first.

# 5

## LEARNING TO EAT NORMALLY AGAIN –
### BEHAVIOUR PROGRAMMES

Many clients believe that once they agree to in-patient programmes for eating disorders, they are either fattened up and shipped out (in the case of anorexia or bulimia) or starved and over-exercised (in the case of obesity). Such extreme punitive approaches, thankfully, no longer exist as part of hospital programmes. They have however been replaced by carefully worked out and managed behaviour programmes which set out to encourage the patient to return to a balanced diet and normal eating habits.

Such behaviour programmes work in two ways. Firstly, they reward patients for positive behaviour such as eating well and secondly they discourage them when they behave destructively. For example when patients refuse to eat their food, they are not allowed access to things they enjoy doing. The system is explained clearly to each patient before the programme begins and a points system is established where each 'contracted' unit of weight gain or loss gets a certain reward in the form of access to desirable activities.

Two aspects of in-patient treatment specific to anorexics and bulimics which may seem like punishment (but are not designed as such) are the imposed use of a bedpan rather than the ward toilets and the blocking up of the wash-basin. Both these measures are in place so as to prevent a bulimic patient from vomiting and an anorexic from disposing of uneaten food. If the ward staff explain the purpose of such rules to the patients, they will usually accept them or even welcome them. In a sense, they come to represent aspects of the secure environment which will help patients in their struggle to change.

At St Francis Medical Centre, eating disorder patients eat in a communal dining area and are asked to remain there for one hour after meals. Under such controlled conditions, it is much easier to monitor patients on a behaviour programme. Approval and disapproval from the medical director can be seen in itself as a reward or punishment by the patients and either encourage or discourage them to keep on trying to improve.

Placing limits on what anorexic patients can or cannot do is usually part of a hospital behavioural programme. In severe cases, they are expected to stay in bed for 24 hours a day. They may not leave their rooms for any purpose. Although this sounds like punishment it has another value. Bed rest has been recommended in the treatment of anorexia nervosa for many decades. Its aims are to reduce energy consumption and to promote weight gain, as well as allowing the nursing staff to keep a close watch on the patient. In time, the patient usually begins to feel secure within the confines of their room which is, in itself, a step towards recovery.

Once patients begin to become involved in their behaviour programme, they are slowly handed back responsibility for their recovery and encouraged to feel powerful in its pursuit. When patients start to gain weight, they are rewarded by being allowed to get up more. Such things as access to newspapers, television, letters, telephone calls and visitors are incorporated into a rewards system. And for those who do not stick to the programme, such things as group therapy and relaxation classes are often withdrawn until they return to the programme.

Often if you ask patients, what kind of 'reward' would encourage them to eat or to reduce their food intake, they will not tell you. On admission to treatment, all the patients at St Francis Medical Centre are assigned a nurse therapist who gets to know them well. The finer aspects of the behaviour programme are worked out in co-operation with this nurse therapist who knows what activities specific patients enjoy most and how they would feel if they weren't allowed to engage in them. For example, if a patient enjoys talking to fellow patients, she will only be allowed to do so if she agrees to follow the behaviour programme.

As we mentioned earlier, the patient must be motivated when agreeing to partake in any form of treatment. It follows then that when a patient agrees to eat and gain weight only to quicken his/her discharge from hospital, this does not mean treatment has been successful. What usually happens in such cases is that once the patient has left the hospital, he/she proceeds to put on or lose weight immediately.

It is only when the nursing staff and dieticians are experienced in dealing with eating disorders and show consistent warm understanding of the patient's plight that weight gain or loss in a hospital setting can be of benefit. Hospital not only offers the patient a safe environment in which to regain health but it can in some cases provide an interruption of the tension – that may have risen to panic level – in the family home.

Rewards and punishments in the hospital environment apply to all patients so that, in contrast to the family situation, the patients in time realise that they are not being singled out. In extreme cases, hospital staff may have to resort to spoon- or even tube-feeding as a life-saving measure. These techniques are, however, rarely necessary and are administered only when the patient has not agreed to partake or is partaking unsuccessfully in a behaviour programme. However, that said, spoon or tube feeding should really only be used as a crisis intervention because it takes away the patient's dignity. Patients are informed of this possibility on admission.

When asked how they feel about such an approach, most patients describe it as the most extreme form of punishment. However, in some cases, anorexics accept tube feeding because it allows them to receive nourishment without having to feel guilty. Some other patients find it reassuring because it makes them feel that the medical team really cares for them to go to such trouble.

Behaviour programmes are seen to be the most appropriate way of dealing with eating disorders by some professionals because patients put on weight more quickly than by other methods. However, letting go of controlling your body through not eating or over-eating is by no means an easy task. While behaviour programmes are efficient in getting the patient to eat normally again, its very efficiency increases the inner turmoil and sense of helplessness among patients. If this is not considered, patients may be discharged as 'medically improved' but psychologically they could become depressed or even suicidal. It is of utmost importance that behavioural treatment is used in conjunction with psychotherapy.

## Learning to Eat Normally Again

To recover from an eating disorder, the patient has to return to normal body weight and keep the weight at this level. Normal body weight is based on a recommended norm for a particular age, sex, height and body build. However it is not enough just to reach a 'target weight'. What is more important is to learn patterns of healthy eating and to maintain a balanced diet. Regaining weight for anorexics and bulimics or losing weight for obese patients is really only half the battle.

A dietician who has experience of working with eating disordered patients is the most appropriate person to teach healthy eating patterns. From the outset a target weight has to be defined for all patients. Many anorexic patients will bring up examples of healthy friends who are much lighter than the average weights in the tables. They will try to bargain about their target weight with the staff members and often try to play one staff member off against another. This form of manipulation by the patient has got to be avoided. Once they are told their target weight, the main concern of overweight persons is how long it will take them to achieve the 'desired weight'.

The patients are weighed twice a week during their hospital stay and usually they are not told which days these are because 'weight days' are often their most anxious days. Patients are asked not to weigh themselves at any other times.

They are encouraged to have a mixed balanced diet, including carbohydrates, eaten at conventional mealtimes. We find it useful for the patients to sit down with the dietician and discuss possible menu items and help to choose foods that they are comfortable eating. Dealing with food in this way allows the patients to play an active role in their recovery.

The dietician will then tell the patient if what they choose is balanced and within their calorie limits. However, a lot of discussion about calories is discouraged. The medical team encourages a slow but consistent weight loss for the obese patients and a gradual weight gain for anorexics and bulimics.

Exercise regimes are also agreed upon. Walking is the most useful exercise for patients recovering from an eating disorder because it doesn't demand over-exertion yet it still provides good overall body movement. Once they begin to partake in a behaviour programme, all patients are allowed to walk.

They are encouraged to attend relaxation classes in the hospital to reduce their anxiety levels. These classes are given by the physiotherapist who also runs special exercise classes for obese patients. The latter are very useful for overweight patients and are carefully designed to prevent any injuries.

While on a behaviour programme, each patient is encouraged to keep a food diary in which to record their feelings before and after eating. An example of such a diary can be seen on the next page.

Getting in touch with the feelings surrounding mealtimes provides useful discussion material for psychotherapy sessions.

Observation of all patients during mealtimes is essential. The obese patients long for mealtime, while it is the most feared time of the day for anorexics and bulimics. If patients are not watched by the staff the obese patients are more than happy to eat for the anorexics or bulimics. Trust between staff and patients is also very important.

Most hospital diets give between 2,500 and 3,000 calories per day. In cases where the anorexic or bulimic patient is extremely anxious about such a 'large' calorific intake, half of these calories can be taken as a fluid form of nutritional preparation rich in protein. Tasty and varied ordinary food should also be offered in conjunction with such supplements to help the patient return to normal eating.

Facing a change is difficult for the eating disorder patient and only the individuals themselves know really the discomfort and panic which eating causes. Not being able to vomit can make the bulimic feel that they are going to gain weight rapidly. The anorexic feels a loss of all control by beginning

| Time | Day | Where | What I ate | Was I hungry | Did food satisfy me? | Feelings prior to eating | Feelings after eating |
|------|-----|-------|-----------|-----|----|-----|-----|
| 7.30 am | Mon. | Kitchen | Cereal, tea, 1 slice brown bread | Yes | Yes | frightened | achievement |
| 1.00 pm | | | Salad sandwich apple | Yes | Yes | didn't want to eat | felt full |
| 5.00 pm | | | vegetable lasagne, salad | No | Too much | didn't want to eat | felt I had over-eaten |

to eat again, while the obese patient has difficulty coping with emotions normally sedated by eating large quantities of food. For this reason, a gradual reduction in calorific intake is recommended for obese patients. Whatever the patient's struggle, the presence of a competent and empathic medical team will motivate and encourage the sufferer to move confidently towards change.

## Eating at Home

Once discharged from hospital, most patients will return to the family home where eating will take place outside the range of professional supervision. Home can be a place of many struggles and conflicts around the matter of eating. Learning to eat normally again is only possible when the anxiety level of the parents and other family members is not too high.

Many parents feel they are the only force with the responsibility of encouraging the patient to 'eat properly and sensibly'. Such feelings of having too much responsibility for what happens next needs to be addressed during family therapy sessions. Parents need to explain to the sufferers that the responsibility for eating lies with themselves. They also need to reassure them that they are at hand if needed to discuss feelings of fear and insecurity or loss of control.

The sufferer needs to fit in with the 'family diet' as much as possible and not be singled out. Contrary to general expectations a diet composed of favourite or special foods may frighten the recovering individuals and make them feel they might lose control again. It is in fact best to pay little heed to food fads developed during the course of the disorder. The difficult task for those close to the sufferer is to keep in mind clear expectations of 'normal' eating of 'normal' food.

Family eating needs to be organised so as to replicate the structure of hospital regimes. Parents and family members need to help the sufferer to separate 'food' arguments from other issues.

Matters of food and weight should not be allowed to predominate in conversation. Parents should avoid saying things like: 'Look at all the trouble I took to prepare your favourite dinner', as this makes the sufferer feel very guilty. Other comments like: 'Do you realise how much this meal cost?' or 'We are all forced to eat your food', do little to improve the situation. They are instead a recipe for the disaster of a future relapse.

Whether the sufferer is treated at out-patient or in-patient level, there is no magic cure. Speed of recovery depends on commitment and struggle for change. Encouraging behavioural changes while simultaneously addressing psychological issues through psychotherapy (which we will deal with in the next chapter) is the most useful combined treatment programme yet devised.

## One Patient's Experience of a Behavioural Programme

Rachel was twenty-four when she agreed to in-patient treatment. She had been anorexic for eight years.

'When I first came to the hospital the thought of eating with the other patients scared the hell out of me. I ate what I wanted to but always alone in my own room. I felt so uncomfortable and panicky. I wanted to make myself sick. I ate slowly and hoped that by some miracle the food would disappear from my plate. I even wore big baggy sleeves in the hope that I could slip the potato up my sleeve.

'Somehow, I struggled on and after about three weeks, it became a little easier. I used to tell my nurse therapist and psychiatrist how I felt. I didn't sleep for a couple of nights thinking of all the food I had eaten but deep down I knew I wanted to get better.

'One day it was so difficult that I just flung the plate onto the floor. I was confined to bed rest for a week after that. It was terrible: I missed the group activities and the company of the other patients. I felt I had been made an example of. I felt caged in. I acted up for three days and then my phone calls and other privileges ceased. In some way, I just wanted to continue punishing myself for eating. I was losing control.

'It was only when the last of my privileges were taken from me that I realised I couldn't go on like this. I didn't want to feel like a rat in a cage. I hated the staff at the time but in hindsight, I realise that they need to take such steps. After all, I was on a destructive path with no desire to change unless somebody was willing to take a risk with me.'

# 6

# GETTING TO THE ROOT
# OF THE ISSUES

Once the patient is medically stable, the next stage in the treatment process is to try to get to the root of the issues behind the eating disorder. As we pointed out earlier, anorexia, bulimia and obesity are only symptoms of something deeper that is going wrong for the individual. Group or individual psychotherapy offers patients a chance to discover and understand what lies behind the eating disorder and how they can learn to cope with their true problems.

Because psychotherapy aims to bring to the surface forgotten memories and hidden fears, it can be a painful process. By its very nature, therapy can bring up emotional issues that patients may have wished away or put to the back of their minds. However, it is often only after such crises are brought back to the surface that the patients can truly understand and cope with their problems.

A psychotherapist is usually a psychologist, doctor or psychiatrist who has undertaken special training. Psychotherapy is a slow process but has proved to be valuable in the treatment of eating disorders. It is however of limited value to patients who are unwilling to participate or to those who find communicating about their feelings too difficult. Psychotherapy is also more difficult for older people because of the mass of experiences they have built up over the years.

At the start of therapy, the therapist takes a detailed personal history and carefully notes any gaps in the patients' account of their lives to date. In general therapists merely listen to the patient; however, they may occasionally direct the patient's thoughts with a word or phrase. Gradually the patient's conversation begins to reveal the repressed matter lying in the unconscious and so helps indicate the origins of the eating disorder.

Some therapists use psychotherapy under hypnosis as it is believed to quicken the process of recovery. However, the success factor is reduced because in this case, it is really the therapist and not the patient who does the 'uncovering'. Dr Moore-Groarke does not practise hypnosis because many patients who had prior experiences of such a treatment approach say that it made them feel out of control. Part of the value of the 'free association' method used in psychotherapy lies in the patients' uncovering hidden memories for themselves.

*The Role of Psychotherapy in the Treatment of Eating Disorders*

In one way or another, patients use their eating disorders to avoid feeling their needs and their pain. Any form of psychotherapy will aim to help the patients let go of their destructive behaviour (the eating disorder) and allow them to feel their hidden emotions. Only then can they begin to understand and work through such emotions. However patients can begin to open up only if they have some form of 'containment' within which they feel safe enough to think about their problems and experience their feelings.

This so-called containment is very important for patients and is usually provided around and within the therapist-patient relationship. The physical boundaries of the consulting room acts as an adequate security for some patients to let them feel comfortable enough to communicate. The confidentiality and professionalism of the therapist is another safe indicator for patients to reveal their true feelings. Gradually a relationship is formed with the therapist within which patients can begin to get in touch with the feeling they have avoided for so long. In time they will also begin to realise that they no longer need to resort to their destructive eating behaviour.

The containment offered by external therapy

sessions is limited and not suitable for all patients. At the end of each session, the patient has to manage alone until the next time. The patient's ability to do this depends on whether s/he can keep the therapist and the focus of the session in mind. Not all patients can do this. Some need a firmer and more continuous form of containment before they can use psychotherapy. Such people can benefit greatly from an in-patient treatment programme like that offered at St Francis Medical Centre in Mullingar. For them, the hospital becomes the necessary container which can be constantly available during their in-patient stay.

During hospital programmes the patient must give up all destructive behaviour. If the patient complies with this rule there will be a flood of painful emotions that up to now were avoided. At this stage, the patient feels unable to tolerate these feelings and what often happens is that s/he pushes them onto others by means of projection. In this way, the patient uses other patients and staff members to carry unwanted feelings of parts of the troubled personality. This process is called splitting.

Splitting has to be addressed in therapy as it can be extremely valuable in directing the patient towards changes in behaviour. Consider the following case:

Ann was a twenty-six year-old anorexic patient. When she first came to group therapy, she was always eager to participate and was doing quite well in terms of opening up and sharing her feelings. When another patient, Sheila, joined the therapy group, there was a marked change in Ann's participation. She clamped up and although her feelings were very visible from her facial expressions, she still refused to speak. On one occasion, she actually started to shake as soon as Sheila joined the group. We addressed this issue later during our individual session and it transpired that Sheila had the same effect on Ann as her older sister.

Another example of splitting arose when one of our patients transferred all her anger onto her nurse therapist. Maeve describes it as follows: 'My nurse therapist became my mother. But I could for once speak my mind to her. I told her how much I disliked her, how I felt she was controlling me and ruining my life by watching my every move.' Maeve soon realised that she always wanted the courage to speak her mind openly to her overprotective mother. The process of splitting also emphasises the necessity of good communication between all members of the medical team so that everyone can be aware of what exactly each patient is experiencing.

One of the tasks I ask all my patients to do during psychotherapy is to build a map of their life. This map is what I call a life chart. It simply asks the patients to go back through their life recording their good and bad memories. I also ask them to complete a family profile by describing their relationships with each other family member. This exercise is a way of gathering the pieces of the jigsaw. During psychotherapy, the pieces of the jigsaw begin to fit together and the picture of the patient's life becomes clearer. (An example of a patient's life chart is shown on the next page.)

Anger is a powerful emotion which needs to be addressed during psychotherapy. One way of doing so is for patients to make a list of people they have felt angry towards during their lives. Describing feelings surrounding the anger and the effect it has on them is also useful. In the following piece, Alice describes her anger towards an uncle who abused her as a child:

'My uncle Tom was seen by all the family to be the "perfect gentleman". Little did my family know that when he used to baby-sit me, he abused me every time He bribed me with sweets and money and threatened to kill me if I ever told anybody of our "secret". I was so frightened. Every time he came near me, I froze. I just tried to block out the harsh reality of what was happening. I used up so much energy trying to block out the abuse I just wasted away. I couldn't eat or sleep. I could never rest and was constantly on the go, always eager to please people for fear that they too would hurt me. It was only when my psychologist asked me, "Was

## LIFE CHART OF: A.X. D.O.B. 14/2/1965

| DATE | 12/11/93 | |
|---|---|---|
| **AGE** | **GOOD MEMORIES** | **BAD MEMORIES** |
| 0–5 | Visiting grandparents house | First day at school |
| | got a puppy called 'Joey' | birth of my brother |
| | my friend's birthday party | my father drowning our cat's kittens |
| | pocket money | our house going on fire |
| | my cuddly teddy bear | being in hospital for 6 weeks |
| | getting some goldfish | being locked under the stairs for stealing sweets |
| | collecting postcards | fear of the dark |
| 6–10 | Christmas mornings | My father's drinking |
| | getting my first bike | arguments between my parents |
| | my first 'Cindy doll' | my grandfather's death |
| | art in school | my father burning my stamps |
| | ballet classes | moving to another town |
| | the school concert | not getting 'lead' in school play |
| 11–15 | Learning piano | My father hitting my mother |
| | clothes and make-up | my uncle abusing me |
| | winning games/school team | my mother in hospital |
| | writing poems | my first period |
| | reading Nancy Drew books | going to secondary school |
| | watching films | losing friends |
| | going to France | exams |
| 16–20 | First disco | My parents splitting up |
| | first boyfriend | anorexia started |
| | first drink | 3 months in hospital |
| | first holiday without my parents | Paul going out with my best friend |
| | parties | getting drunk too often |
| | recovering from anorexia | taking anti-depressants |
| 21–25 | Meeting Harry | First sexual experience |
| | moving out of home | getting pregnant |
| | buying first car | being out of work for 6 months |
| | first job | overdose/being pumped out |
| | promotion at work | miscarriage |
| | holidays abroad | one night stands |
| 26–30 | Getting married | Affair |
| | buying a home | Mark threatening to leave me |
| | birth of my son | return of anorexia |
| | resolving anorexia for good | fear of pregnancy |
| | learning to trust again | hospital admissions |

I always happy to put others needs before my own?" that I began to allow my anger towards Tom come to the surface. Up until then, I could literally feel the anger coming up towards my neck but then I would push it back down. The abuse affected my whole life. I was scared to develop a relationship with a man. I was frightened to mix socially. I feared rejection above anything else in my life. I felt guilty for allowing the abuse to take place in the first instance. I turned the anger I had towards Tom inwards on myself. I essentially put my life on hold.'

Writing is a powerful tool that can help the psychotherapeutic process. It can act as a preparation for the next session or a follow-up from the last. Writing letters can also be useful for patients as a means of saying goodbye to a deceased member of the family. Letters to a perpetrator of abuse or to someone the patient has difficulty with or even a self-directed letter of forgiveness can act as an exercise of self-confrontation as well as letting go negative feelings. Letters are often read out during therapy sessions and may even provide matter for role-playing. The system provides the patient with a mechanism for confronting the person in the letter. Here is an example of such a letter:

Dear Mum,
I have been asked by my psychologist to write a

letter to you letting you know how I feel about the relationship we had. All my life I felt as if I had been wrapped up in cotton wool. I was never allowed to develop into my own person. You pushed me academically and my achievements were all that ever mattered to you. I did well at school but the fact that I was overweight appalled you. You will remember that there was very little physical affection in our home. I can never remember you telling me that you loved me.

As a child if I was good or 'did well' you always rewarded me with sweets. As I grew older, I used that same reward to block out my feelings of loneliness and isolation. I ate my way through my frustrations. I hated being an only child. I hated the way you never allowed me to talk about the fact that I was adopted. How I wished that some day I would find my real mother but living here in Ireland made that difficult.

I wonder did you realise how you were also controlling my father. Little wonder that he remarried eighteen months after your death. How happy he appears now; the freedom in life without you is so great. I dress the way I want. I choose my own friends. I don't feel forced to go to church and yes, at last, I am doing something about my weight. I feel since I started therapy that I have been given a new lease of life, a second chance of reliving my youth.

I wish things could have been different between us. I hope I never marry a woman like you. You must have had a very repressive childhood. I wonder did you ever love me or my father. Goodbye, mother, you can see now that we can survive without you. You are no longer here to put us on one of your guilt trips.

Life is worth living. It's sad that you couldn't see that.

Your adopted son,

James

In therapy, it is also necessary to get in touch with the 'inner child'. To do this the therapist usually asks the patient to try to describe what s/he was like, for example at the start of school? (This is usually a child's first experience of separation from the parents and home environment). The client may be asked to describe feelings when new babies came along or to give childhood memories of parents and the like.

American psychotherapist, Louise Hay, stresses the importance of getting in touch with the 'inner child' to enhance emotional growth. If this doesn't happen the eating disorder patient often stays stuck emotionally at the age of onset of the illness or associated life event crisis.

Patients with eating disorders can also have a personality disorder. In the last number of years, I have come across three patients who have also had multiple-personality disorders. With such a condition, patients revert to childlike personalities. They are often confused about their identity and seem not to remember things. Multiple-personality disorder differs from other psychiatric syndromes in that the patient has two or more relatively consistent but alternating identities as well as recurrent episodes of memory distortion and complete memory loss.

One such case is Kelly who acts out a personality which she calls 'little Kelly' who is seven. This seven-year-old personality coincides with the time Kelly was first abused by her brother. Another personality, 'Stephanie', who is nineteen, represents the destructive part of Kelly's behaviour. The fact that 'Stephanie' is nineteen is also significant in that it was the age of the onset of Kelly's bulimia.

### Recurring Issues in Psychotherapy for People with Eating Problems

*(a) The patient says very little during therapy sessions*
During therapy, patients turn up regularly but often say very little. Only after long silences do they offer fragments of information. When this happens, the patient often complains about having nothing to say or asks the therapist to direct the course of the session by introducing specific topics.

Such an attitude towards therapy usually means that 'secret' patterns of behaviour are occurring. For example, the obese patient may still be anaesthetising emotions by comfort eating, the bulimic patient may be vomiting to get rid of negative feelings or the anorexic patient may be limiting dietary intake for fear of losing control.

If such silences continue another form of treatment such as art therapy can be useful – if the patient is willing. When patients are asked to draw a picture of how they are feeling, the representation and the colours tell a million stories.

Although patients are asked if they have a history of sexual abuse, some don't give straight answers. One patient asked if she could draw during therapy and in most of her drawings a hand kept appearing. In time she revealed that she had been abused and that the hand in her drawings was, in fact, the hand of her abuser.

*(b) The patient wants to talk about food all the time*
During the early sessions of psychotherapy, patients often try to talk a lot about dieting, food intake, body size and fatness. This subject has been the main item of the patient's conscious mind for a long time and it would be surprising if it were not to appear in therapy. However, at a symbolic level, through talking about food, patients are trying to tell the therapist how bad they feel about them-

selves. They are also signalling that they are afraid of the emotional upheaval that will ensue if they let go of their crutch. In a sense, patients reject the therapist's 'mental food' as firmly as they reject 'body food' from a parent or staff member in a hospital.

If therapy is to be of value, food must be de-emphasised from the outset. If this doesn't happen the patients will continue to use the crutch upon which their lives are dependant. Some therapists find it useful to set out specific ground rules before therapy can begin. Usually a written contract between patient and therapist is the best means of overcoming any conflict resulting from the lack of permission to use the sessions to discuss the 'food obsession'. I remember one such case vividly when a patient disguised her anorexia as an inability to taste and smell which meant that all medical possibilities had to be explored. Eventually, it became necessary to stop all discussion of such a possibility, even in family therapy.

*(c) The patient does not want to take back responsibility for his/her life*

At some point the therapist must stand back from the patient, both from a wish for life and health for the patient and from the professional need to cure and not to fail. We must make patients aware that the responsibility for recovery lies with them and that the therapist is merely a catalyst.

If the patient is unaware of this responsibility for recovery, therapists may find themselves being manipulated. Sometimes patients subtly try to provoke the parent or therapist into becoming the 'demanding greedy child' who needs something rather than the other way around.

Therapists are often placed in the position where they are damned if they do and damned if they don't! They, however, must not allow the patient to see their concern if the patient is failing to make progress, otherwise the patient may act up. A good relationship with the patient's doctor or psychiatrist is necessary so that medical care can be set up quickly and easily if required.

Patients must be made to realise that as well as other people wanting them to recover they must want recovery for themselves. In the chapter on 'Admitting the Problem', we acknowledged that this first step involves a certain amount of risk-taking. This taking of responsibility also reinforces our assertion that the treatment philosophy should involve the patient's playing an active role in recovery.

*(d) The patient is over-conforming*

There are occasions when therapy seems to be anxiety-free. When this happens, it should set alarm bells ringing. When the patient is always pleasant and co-operative, agreeing with everything the therapist says, this is often an indicator that all is not well. The therapist will soon realise that the patient has created a kind of false therapy where there is no need to address any of the problems such as fear of failing in an exam, of leaving home or forming intimate sexual relationships.

What is essentially happening in such cases is that the patients are behaving like young children who believe that if they conform, everything will be all right. This is usually the case with victims of sexual abuse: 'If I conform, the abuse will soon be over.'

Successful psychotherapy like any development in life is never a smooth process. The path to recovery is full of twists and turns and even cul de sacs. It is however the trust and rapport between therapist and client that eventually shows the way out of the tunnel towards the light and the means of regaining an appropriate way of living and the quality of life that all of us deserve.

Eating-disorder patients are starved of understanding yet terrified that if they allow themselves to begin to want to change, something dreadful will happen. Psychotherapy has to be accompanied by other support and treatment as these patients have a real and alarming capacity for self-destructive behaviour. The impulse to damage the self and to sabotage the therapy must be carefully addressed by the medical team in charge.

By the end of therapy, the patient has to be convinced that the therapist is an understanding person who is strong and reliant enough to see how destructive the patient's behaviour with respect to food can be. The patient must have confidence that the therapist is not going to be thrown into a panic no matter what the result of the patient's behaviour.

The therapist needs to be very patient to see patients through the various stages of treatment. There is no quick recovery for any of the eating disorders. Anorexia, bulimia and obesity are disorders which affect the person's whole personality and sense of self. The therapist must be prepared and able to provide an atmosphere in which the patients can discover or re-discover who they really are. Our ideal for treatment is *mens sana in corpore sano* – 'a healthy mind is a healthy body'.

# 7

# CRISIS POINTS IN RECOVERY
## HIDDEN VULNERABILITIES IN THE FUTURE

We all face hidden vulnerabilities in our lives that we can not control. Such things as the loss of a job, financial difficulties, the death of a loved one, a car crash, terminal illness, the break-up of a relationship and miscarriage are all happenings that generally speaking we cannot predict or prevent. We all handle stressful life events in different ways but for those recovering from an eating disorder, such events can lead to a relapse or a return to their destructive behaviour. For some bulimics or anorexics, the ordinary everyday trials of life can be enough to bring on a relapse.

Anyone who is working towards change while recovering from an eating disorder, has to learn to deal with crisis points. Apart from being triggered by an acute life stress like one of those mentioned above, a relapse can also come about because of the failure to resolve or admit to a significant issue earlier in therapy. This occasionally happens with some patients who deny sexual abuse during the initial therapy sessions. Such patients end up 'hanging on' to the issue rather than dealing with it through the appropriate steps and in the safe environment established between therapist and patient.

The key to real recovery is 'quick recovery after relapse'. For this to happen, patients must admit they have relapsed and ask for help sooner rather than later. Patients cannot however suffer a relapse if they have not yet begun the process of recovery.

### What Are the Signs of a Relapse?

The signs of relapse are exactly the same as the mood swings and destructive behaviour characteristic of the original problem. However, the patient and sometimes the family denies the recurrence of such symptoms because they don't want to believe the patient's condition has deteriorated. Family members are as likely to deny a relapse as the patients themselves because they usually see it as a reflection of their own inadequacies in dealing with the problem.

The sufferers' eating problems get back into the driving seat and they come to believe that life can be managed by food alone. The patient again denies the existence of the eating disorder or questions whether it is truly addictive after all.

Unless approached in a caring manner, patients in relapse will retreat back into their cocoon. All the old feelings of guilt, anger, shame, low self-esteem and low self-confidence reappear. They feel unworthy, helpless, confused and afraid. There is a strong feeling of being caught in a 'catch-22' situation where admitting the relapse is as bad as that of denying its existence.

Maeve was one such patient who described the guilt she felt when she first relapsed. 'I had been in therapy for almost a year. I had lost three and a half stone and felt I was really getting my life together. I had worked on my whole family relationships, and in particular the awful episodes of sexual abuse by my uncle. During my time as an in-patient, I can remember the psychiatrist saying to me that he had a suspicion that I may have been abused by my own father. I denied this profusely and six months later, when I had a few days off work, strange thoughts came flooding back to me, completely out of the blue.

'I couldn't believe I was having these thoughts. I wanted to ignore them. I felt completely out of control as far as my feelings were concerned. In order to suppress these feelings, I started to overeat once more. I felt caught in a "catch-22" situation: neither of the options open to me was appealing – I could sedate my feelings by overeating or I could allow myself to open up again and feel vulnerable. It was too easy to remember how difficult it was dealing with my uncle's abuse. I was afraid I couldn't go through that again. I really had "a fear of fear". I ignored my therapist and built up a barrier between us. For me, this was my first relapse.'

Often during a relapse, patients replace their eating abuse with another addiction; for example the obese person may start drinking excessively, the bulimic may start over-exercising or the anorexic may become a workaholic. This means that their minds have never been sufficiently clear of the process of addiction to be at any significant stage of recovery. When patients stop eating, induce vomiting or go on a binge, they can often be found to be making plans for someone else's recovery, thus directing the attention away from themselves. This makes them feel they are not relapsing.

Patients who have relapsed are still suffering greatly. They still believe that they can control food. They have not yet accepted the defeat that is the essential component of any recovery programme. To recover from an eating disorder, patients need to surrender their power over food. It is only by finally admitting defeat that sufferers are able to see that there is hope for recovery once more.

Some people never admit defeat. When a therapist confronts them about this, they will react by not attending the next session. When we suggested a re-admission to in-patient programme for some patients, we received comments like 'Oh doctor, I couldn't go back again. That would be a real sign of failure', or 'What would the staff think of me? After all, I was doing so well'. This period is a crucial one in therapy. Often it is more difficult to re-engage a client in an in-patient programme than it was to involve them initially when they admitted to the eating disorder.

Parents or friends should never be afraid to voice their suspicions about relapses or possible relapses. If family members were more vigilant, re-engaging a patient in an in-patient programme would be easier. For many sufferers, the first relapse often occurs during their first weekend home. This is partly because patients in an intensive in-patient programme have a real fear of becoming 'institutionalised'. Their first return visit home can lead them to believe that they will never fit in again. This is why it is crucial that staff address such possibilities before and after the visit. A therapist has to use clinical judgement about delaying a visit home if a relapse is likely to lead the patient to run away from their attempts at recovery.

Some sufferers never surrender but try to remain 'in control' of their food disorder. Sadly, some people die as a result of their addiction before even beginning to recover. Others prefer to continue with the 'familiar eating disorder' rather than accept the need for personal change. Change is seen by many sufferers to be more painful than continuing with the addiction. However, the longer a patient continues to live with eating disorders, the more likely they are to suffer permanent damage.

For some female sufferers, anorexia or bulimia begins or recurs during pregnancy. Bulimia is more difficult to detect during pregnancy as it is often passed off as morning sickness. The development of an eating disorder during pregnancy is thought to be linked to the inability to cope with the bodily changes. Usually, these cases occur when the sufferer is already in her twenties and some of the pregnancies come to full-term despite the illness.

Women with less severe cases or those in the recovery phase of a more severe case may become pregnant even while still amenorrhoeic (without their monthly periods). Some of these pregnancies, too, come to term, especially if there is some weight gain. The risks to the foetus and mother are increased, however, and it is generally recommended that such patients wait until recovery is well established before becoming pregnant.

On the other hand, many anorexics and bulimics will eat and not induce vomiting so as to nourish the baby during pregnancy and yet within six weeks of delivery will return to a more severe form of their condition. Anorexics and bulimics usually have babies with lower birth weights, less weight gain and with more foetal complications. In some cases, these complications result in the death of the foetus.

Oonagh had had anorexia since her early teens and according to her family, she had made a complete recovery before she got married and had her two children. However, both pregnancies were extremely difficult and Oonagh spent quite some time in hospital before the babies were born. Following each pregnancy, she became severely anorexic. She had conceived both her babies against medical advice and she is still anorexic although she refuses to admit this. Oonagh fools herself into believing her life is complete with her husband, nice home and two young children. Only she can decide when the time is right to examine her anorexia. It is to be hoped that she will before it is too late for herself and her family.

Recovery from an eating disorder is possible for anyone who wants it regardless of how much has been lost or damaged – short of physical damage to the brain itself. Sufferers are never too old or too young, too early in their problem or too late, to begin recovery when they truly want it. Some people sadly continue to suffer with their food disorder to death (one such case was Karen Carpenter). Even while making repeated attempts to recover, they suffer relapses time and time again. Often, such patients choose suicide rather than the continuing pain or recurrent relapses. Families and professionals also find it difficult to accept that some people cannot make that personal decision towards recovery. As professionals, all we can do is carry the offer and message of recovery.

## How Can Sufferers Protect Themselves from Relapse?

Only by learning the addictive nature of eating disorders can sufferers help themselves to recover. This involves understanding that there is always a possibility of relapse and that it is important continually to monitor their condition. The following are ways in which this can be done.

*1:* Having access to a professional who will act as a mirror, reflecting back the attitudes and behaviour of the sufferers is a useful means of understanding the problem. The professional will also help the sufferer to gain personal insight and to establish goals for improvement and quick recovery from relapse.

*2:* Listening to feedback from professionals and group members (if the patient is attending group therapy) is also a useful way of monitoring progress. Feedback can sometimes be resented by sufferers but it is a positive aid if given in an open, honest and non-judgmental manner.

*3:* Taking part in stress-management courses helps to enhance confidence levels and coping skills for those recovering from an eating disorder. Most inpatient and out-patient programmes now offer these courses.

**4:** Becoming aware of one's own particular risks of cross-addiction and avoiding such substances and behaviours are other useful steps towards recovery. As we said earlier, some patients replace the food addiction with over-exercising, alcohol, drugs or overwork. Sufferers are also most vulnerable when tired, lonely, angry or, in the case of overeaters, hungry.

**5:** Following simple recommendations such as recording your feelings before and after eating and using relaxation techniques. Ringing your therapist when you are feeling down can also be helpful in monitoring progress. An important admonition for the sufferer is: 'Don't return to the food without at least asking yourself: "Why are you doing this?"' There is always a more positive coping strategy. Taking each day as it comes and remembering that support is available is a useful maxim. All our patients sign a contract at the beginning of therapy to use the 'phone-in facility' if they feel they are going to suffer a relapse. It is also important for this reason that patients have a good relationship with their doctor.

**6:** Establishing protection mechanisms such as family get-togethers or meetings with a trusted friend can act as a form of insurance for those in recovery. Always carrying the therapist's and general practitioner's telephone numbers is another reassurance. However, all patients must remember that it is they who are responsible for addressing the relapse as it is up to them to decide whether to recover continually from their eating disorder.

## How Does One Intervene in Relapse?

The truthful answer to this question is that it is very difficult to know exactly when to intervene, particularly if all you can be certain of is that the sufferer may return to their old behaviour.

Clearly, the earlier the intervention takes place the better but, whether family member or professional, one has to be extremely cautious so as not to imagine a relapse that is not really occurring.

Intervention should therefore be initiated only on clear evidence (for example, food missing from the kitchen, signs of vomiting by the patient, drinks missing from the cabinet, aggressive mood swings) supported by others, either professional or other family members. Anyone who does intervene should do so in a caring and understanding manner, respecting the dignity of the patient.

In our hospital programme if we feel that a patient is near relapse or has already 'acted out' intention of relapse, the matter is first talked out at the team meeting before discussing it with the patient. Likewise in the family milieu, it might be more useful for the parents to call a family therapy session in conjunction with the therapist. Sometimes, the therapist will see the family members who have voiced their suspicions, before meeting with the patient.

The sufferer who has had a late relapse may be surprised to be asked to re-attend for weekly therapy. However, it is important to stress to the patient that this is not a retrograde step and there should be no sense of failure in undergoing further treatment. Talking to other sufferers who have already been through the process of relapse can also help. What needs to be addressed is the approach to food. We all have to admit that though we do not have control over life events we can control our reaction to them.

Once sufferers have admitted their powerlessness over food, they have taken the first step back on the road to recovery. Perhaps the most significant recommendation in all recovery programmes is that one should aim for progress rather than perfection. Remember, 'if at first you don't succeed, try, try again'. Eating disorders signal to sufferers that they are in control, that they are 'special and different' and that 'all problems in their lives are external'. The process of recovery is essentially one of reversing this process and accepting that all true recovery and change come from within.

# 8

# TAKING CONTROL

By now you should now realise the complexity of all three eating disorders. Recognising the need to change the approach to food, takes time. Motivation is the key to success. Recovery is a long and difficult path for most sufferers and their families. Many patients have to learn to deal with periods of relapse, as was discussed in the last chapter, and we have no control over our hidden vulnerabilities in the future.

Taking control of a food addiction means learning to grow up. There is no easy panacea. When treatment begins the sufferer is no older than at the age of onset of the condition and you cannot expect to grow up and mature overnight.

When you let go of your defences you feel exposed, weak and vulnerable. Each time somebody insensitively asks you 'Why can't you eat normally?' you feel angry and upset. If only things were as simple as that. How many times have you been told to cop yourself on or had your appearance criticised. Such statements do nothing for your self-esteem. And then as the battle continues you have to learn to deal with people telling you how well you look! Then you start questioning yourself all over again. When anorexics or bulimics are told that they are looking well, they may feel they are putting on too much weight. Obese patients may interpret such a statement as a licence to binge. Sensitivity is required at all stages of treatment and recovery.

Sufferers may feel that changes in family dynamics are too slow. They have to realise that one can only change oneself. The other members of the family have got to opt for change for themselves and sometimes they never manage it.

The sufferer never wants to hear the word 'diet' again. The word 'diet' has a punitive connotation and highlights all that is negative in the personality: weak will-power, lack of discipline, eating in private followed by huge denial. The word 'diet' will reinforce these negative images. They thus become self-fulfilling prophecies. The word should be replaced with 'healthy eating plan'.

Taking control of an eating disorder means correctly diagnosing the cause and identifying some of the contributing factors. Several causes and contributing factors have been put forward throughout this book. Once the real enemy (not the food) has been identified, patients can harness and transfer their energies positively to correct it.

Successful treatment programmes approach

anorexia, bulimia and obesity in a positive way by emphasising the positive attributes in the patient's nature. The patient should take stock of his or her good points – sincerity, humour, loyalty, good social skills and use them creatively, positively and not destructively. One of the first exercises in therapy should be to list these positive attributes. Patients always find it easier to list their negative attributes. They say they feel fat, ugly, etc. Usually negative attributes are food- or weight-related.

When under stress, it is important for the sufferer to try to develop a positive alternative (for example going for a walk, ringing a friend etc.) to compete with the enticing and all too familiar enemies: bingeing, purging or in the case of the anorexic, refusing to eat. If the choice under stress is between the enemy (food) or nothing, quite obviously the tendency will be towards the former.

If on the other hand, the choice is between food and control, it is seen as a proper choice. If anything the destructive images of food will begin to fade in comparison to the images associated with the transfer of the control to the patient on the road to recovery. The food prescription takes on a new role. The trick is to develop a positive self-image. This will require some thought, discussion, imagination, concentration, learning and practice. But, it is indeed within any motivated sufferer's grasp.

### Rules for Weight Control for All Sufferers

*1:* *Eat balanced meals.* The dietician will help you identify what constitutes healthy, well-balanced meals.

*2:* *Eat only from a plate* and sit down when you are eating. This will encourage you to have a relaxed approach to eating and help you to avoid picking as you cook. Never eat at the fridge or watching television.

*3:* *Always have some healthy snacks available.* It is useful to work on these but with your dietician.

*4:* *Never eat in secret.* Most overweight people do most of their eating in secret and in company only eat small meals. Always try to eat with a family member or friend. Anorexics and bulimics usually feel very uncomfortable eating in front of other people.

*5:* *Minimise your alcohol intake* to avoid cross addiction.

*6:* *Identify the real cause of your problem.* Remember as we stated, food is only a symptom of the real disorder.

*7:* *Develop alternative rewards for yourself.* In other words make a list of non-food treats such as a new haircut, a new dress, going to a film, etc.

*8:* *Always stick to a shopping list* and make it out before going to the supermarket.

*9:* *Start now,* don't wait for your impending ill-

health or when things get so bad that you want to
end it all.

**10:** *Consult your GP for further advice.*

Another part of taking control is learning how to
socialise or entertain without feeling you are going
to lose control. Forward planning is the key here.
Again this is an issue which should be discussed
with your dietician. A built-in break-out might be
giving yourself permission to have your favourite
foods for a special occasion such as a wedding, an-
niversary or birthday. Built-in break-outs, however,
often lead to relapse, especially for the obese
patient.

### Moderation Is the Key

When you are eating, you should try to enjoy your
food. You will not panic about food, if you learn to
eat slowly. If you are preparing the food take care
to make an attractive presentation. As you recover
from your eating disorder, you will find that once
you have finished eating you will think no more
about the food. Life should not be a case of 'I wake
to eat, or I sleep to eat'. A real sign of recovery is
that you can stop thinking of food. It no longer con-
trols you, when you can control what you eat.

Counting calories should no longer be an obsession. Once you learn healthy eating patterns you

need never again refer to the number of calories you consume. If you find your weight gain or weight loss has reached a plateau for more than two weeks, then it becomes imperative to find out what the problem is.

It is also very important for you to have some of your favourite foods on occasions. These should be seen as a reward and taken preferably when everybody else is having the same thing. Moderation is a very important concept.

Really what you need to learn is normal eating habits and lifestyle habits improving the overall quality of your life. Food should be one of your pleasures but not your only one. Your time is too valuable to waste on just this aspect of your life.

## *Nutrition Counselling*

Part of Dr Moore-Groarke's assessment procedure involves patients filling out a Nutrition Counselling questionnaire. The questions asked are as follows:

1: (a) What foods did you eat as a child?
   (b) What foods did you like?
   (c) What foods did you dislike?

2: (a) Which of those foods do you still eat?
   (b) List some foods you hated as a child and that you eat now.

       (c) List some foods you liked that you don't
          eat now.

    *3:* (a) Which foods were special treats in your
          childhood?
      (b) What activities and people were involv-
          ed when you had these special
          treats?
      (c) How do you feel about these foods then
          and now?

    *4:* (a) How else has your diet changed?
      (b) What is your present diet like?

    *5:* What would you like to change about your
         present diet?

Once patients are seen to be taking control, they are asked to fill out this questionnaire again and the two sets of answers are compared. Patients who have adopted a healthy approach to eating will no longer feel guilty about eating favourite foods. They will no longer substitute a meal for one portion of a favourite food. They may even notice that they now eat foods that they were afraid to eat during their illness. The recovering patient shows less panic and rigidity when the questionnaires are compared.

    Most patients are relieved to learn that with

proper education they can learn to eat normally again. They become less concerned about their basic metabolic rate (BMR) – the calories that you burn off at rest all day, just to have your heart beating and lungs pumping. Some people have a higher BMR and seem to be able to eat anything and not get fat – the 'greyhound breed' – but whatever your BMR you have to live with it. The only way to increase your metabolism is to increase your exercise each day but as with eating, exercise must also be taken in moderation and discussed with your doctor prior to you starting any regime.

*Some Guidelines for Exercising*

When choosing exercise, it is important to try and pick an activity that you enjoy and is practical for you. You must be able to build your exercise plan into your daily routine. Do not make it too difficult for yourself. Obese patients in particular have to choose their exercise activity very carefully, because otherwise they may injure hips, knees, arches and the spine.

Walking is perhaps the most useful exercise of all. Swimming is also recommended. Riding a bicycle for patients who dislike walking is quite safe.

Always remember: once you choose an exercise regime, take the same precautions as any athlete would, such as careful warm-up and cool-down stretching procedures. Yoga is particularly useful for anorexic patients as it also helps them to relax. The physiotherapist has a very important role to play in discussing exercise regimes, especially for physically handicapped or disabled patients.

Control of your life following an eating disorder should allow you to enjoy yourself, feeling more confident in yourself and your new image. You should not be thinking about food for any greater time than it takes to prepare and eat your meals. If you are thinking about food more often than this, then you have not learned much and are likely to go right back to the same old destructive patterns.

Remember you should fight your eating disorder not simply for the sake of aesthetics, but for your physical and psychological health. All three eating disorders will shorten your life span and take from the enjoyment of living. If you correct the eating disorder at a physical and psychological level, you will live longer. You will also become an easier person to live with, because you will be less self-enmeshed.

You will also be able to function in a more mature manner and find that you no longer have to isolate yourself from family or friends. Once you take control there are so many things in life that you can aim for. One obese woman once said in therapy, 'Once I accepted what I was doing to myself, I realised how selfish I was to deny my husband and children the pleasure of my company'. When socialising you will choose healthy foods and no longer have to go to a restaurant before a night out and study the menu as many anorexics and bulimics have done.

Just for the sake of absent-minded bingeing, purging or starvation, eating-disorder sufferers give up so much of their lives. The constant bombardment with media images emphasising beauty and thinness represents a sharp contrast for most people. Your own sense of self-worth sinks even lower if you are trying to compare yourself with the illusions of the silver screen. Your only question should be 'Am I the best I am capable of being?'

Whether you think you can or can't change, ultimately the choice is yours. There is help out there for those who want it.

# APPENDIX

The following is a list of some of the places where treatment is available if you believe you or a member of your family are suffering from an eating disorder. It is advisable first of all, to contact your GP who may be able to put you in touch with a local professional or some source of help in your area.

1.  **St Francis Medical Centre**
    Ballinderry
    Mullingar
    Co Westmeath.
    Tel: 044-41500

Private Hospital, treats all eating disorders. Special Dietary Disorder Unit within a general hospital. They also run a number of out-patient clinics:

> Contact: Dr Edmond Holland, Consultant Psychiatrist or Mrs Emer Hyland, Ward Manager.

(a) St Francis Counselling Service
    32 Crumlin Rd.
    Dublin 12.
    Tel: 01-4540559

Contact: Mr John Riordan, Counsellor.

(b)  St Francis Medical Out-patient Centre
1 Shanakiel Park
Sundays Well
Cork.
Tel: 021-302050
Contact: Dr Gillian Moore-Groarke,
Director/Consultant Psychologist.

2.  **Eating Disorder Unit**
St Patrick's Hospital
James Street
Dublin 8.
Tel: 01 775423
Private psychiatric hospital.
Contact: Dr John Griffin, Psychiatrist/
Clinical Director or Mr Gerard Butcher,
Programme Manager.

3.  **Dr Anne Leader,**
Bons Secours Hospital
Dublin.
Tel: 01-360660
Private practitioner/consultant psychiatrist
in eating disorders.

4.  **Overeaters Anonymous (OA)**
Tel: 01-2694800; ext. 250 for your local

contact.

The organisation is open to anorexics and bulimics as well as overeaters.

5. **Weight Watchers Ireland,**
   1 Phibsborough Rd.
   Dublin 7.
   Tel 01-306511
   The organisation is open to anybody trying to lose weight in a healthy fashion. Classes are run throughout the country.
   Contact: Mrs Rita Fagan

6. **St Vincent's Hospital**
   Elm Park
   Dublin 4.
   Tel: 01-2694533
   Four public beds available for eating disorders.
   Contact: Dr Mary Darby

7. **Unislim**
   49 Dorset St. Lower
   Dublin 1.
   Tel: 01-8740794 for your local class.

8. **Citizens Advice Bureau**
   Tel: 01-331687
   Your local CAB often carries a list of

practitioners/counselling services special-
ising in the treatment of eating disorders.

9.  **Your local health board** may be able to help
    with a list of specialised practitioners.

    Eastern Health Board          01-6790700
    Midland Health Board          0506-21868
    Mid Western Health Board      061-316655
    North Eastern Health Board    046-40341
    North Western Health Board    072-55123
    South Eastern Health Board    056-51702
    Southern Health Board         021-545011
    Western Health board          091-751131

10. **Irish Psychological Society**
    13 Adelaide Rd.
    Dublin 2.
    Tel: 01-783916
    Gives a list of registered psychologists
    throughout the country, some of whom may
    have experience and an interest in eating
    disorders.

11. **Irish Association of Counselling**
    9 Tivoli Tce. East
    Dun Laoghaire
    Co Dublin.
    Tel: 01-2844752

Gives a list of accredited counsellors.

12. **Eating Disorder Association**
    Bryson House
    38 Ormeau Rd.
    Belfast 7.
    Tel: 080232-234914
    13 centres throughout Northern Ireland.
    Self-help groups and individual therapy for
    sufferers of anorexia, bulimia and their
    families.
    Contact: Paul Caughey.

13. **Eating Disorder Association,**
    Sackville Pl.
    44 Magdelen St.
    Norwich
    Norfolk NR3 IJE
    Britain.
    By becoming a member you receive infor-
    mation and copies of their magazine *Sign-
    post*.
    Contact: Angela Wright.

14. **Hazelden Ireland**
    P.O. Box 616
    Cork.
    Hazelden provide useful literature on cop-
    ing with eating disorders. Their approach is

mainly a twelve-step programme.

*N.B. Some services will be covered by your local health board, or you may be able to claim benefit from private medical insurance schemes. Many therapists operate a sliding scale fee system, so do not be afraid to ask. It is your responsibility to check the credentials of your therapist.*

The above list is published for information purposes only. As not every form of treatment is suitable for all people it would be prudent and advisable to consult with a general practitioner before embarking on any course of treatment. Dr Moore-Groarke will not accept patient referrals without a general practitioner's letter.

## More Interesting Books

# An Easy Guide to Meditation

### Roy Eugene Davis

Meditation is the natural process to use to release tension, reduce stress, increase awareness, concentrate more effectively and be open to life. In this book you will learn how to meditate correctly for inner growth and spiritual awareness. Specific guidelines are provided to assist the beginner as well as the more advanced meditator. Here are proven techniques used by accomplished meditators for years: *prayer, mantra, sound-light contemplation, ways to expand consciousness and to experience transcendence.*

Benefits of correct meditation practice include: deep relaxation, stress reduction, inner calm, improved powers of intelligence, and strengthening of the immune system. People in all walks of life can find here the keys to living life as it was meant to be lived.

*Over 100,000 copies sold.*

# Body-Mind Meditation
# A Gateway to Spirituality

## Louis Hughes

You can take this book as your guide for a fascinating journey that need not take you beyond your own hall door. For it is an inward journey, and it will take you no further than God who, for those who want him as a friend, lives within. On the way to God-awareness, you will be invited to experience deep relaxation of body and mind.

*Body-Mind Meditation* can help you become a more integrated balanced person. It is an especially helpful approach to meditation if the pace of life is too fast for you, or if you find yourself frequently tense or exhausted.

# The Spirit of Tony de Mello

## A Handbook of Meditation Exercises

### John Callanan

This book captures the essence and spirit of Tony de Mello. He was a great teacher. Some said he was a dangerous one. He constantly challenged himself, the world within which he lived and those he came into contact with. For some this element of challenge was both unsettling and confusing. Tony said that our security does not lie in thoughts or ideas no matter how profound. Neither does it lie in traditions – no matter how hallowed. Security can only reside in an attitude of mind and a readiness to reflect deeply, thus subjecting any and every belief to rigorous questioning.

So Tony urged people to question, question, question. Questions often make us uncomfortable. They do, however, force us to reflect and thus ensure our growth.

John Callanan has started the book with an opening chapter on the basics of prayer. Then he moves on to try and give a flavour of the ideas and themes which gave so much zest and life to Tony de Mello's presentations. The exercises in this book are based on the prayer-style which Tony himself developed during his retreats.